Praise for
The Collapse of Distinction

"*Collapse of Distinction* is further evidence that Scott McKain is the premiere business communicator of our time. Not only has Scott produced extraordinary results in his own businesses by adhering to these principles, but he makes it simple for you to do so as well. By following the easily applied concepts from *Collapse of Distinction*, you will set the standard of excellence for your industry and make your competition irrelevant."

> — **Joseph Michelli, PhD,**
> speaker, consultant, and author of *The Starbucks Experience*

"Differentiation is not an option in business. In a world where the word 'commodity' has become the norm, Scott McKain clarifies the all-important (and all-profitable) strategy to become *different*, become *distinct*, and become *dominant* in your marketplace. Buy this book. Read it. And put it into practice. "

> — **Jeffrey Gitomer,**
> author of *The Little Red Book of Selling*

"Scott McKain's latest book, *Collapse of Distinction*, is a *must-read* for any professional or organization attempting to creatively differentiate from the competition."

> — **Don Hutson,**
> co-author of the #1 *New York Times* bestseller *The One Minute Entrepreneur*, and CEO of U. S. Learning

"Scott McKain's *Collapse of Distinction* may just save our sanity and common sense with his positive approach to business and life itself."

> — **Joe Bonsall,**
> thirty-five year member of legendary music group, The Oak Ridge Boys, and author of the best-selling book *G.I. Joe and Lillie.*

"With superb style, storytelling, and rationale, *Collapse of Distinction* is a distinctive piece of business and personal literature."

— **Ty Boyd,**
Founder and Chairman, Executive
Learning Systems

"If I can't tell the difference between you and your competitor, why should I spend my money with you? Scott McKain's new book teaches how to answer that question—the *right* way!"

— **Larry Winget,**
television personality and *New York Times*
best-selling author of *People Are Idiots and
I Can Prove It*

"*Collapse of Distinction* isn't just a business success book, this is a business *survival* book for the reality of today's marketplace. If customers don't see what makes you different, then you're just a commodity—forced to live or die on price alone. Lucky for us, McKain shows the way to differentiation through strategies that create distinction—generating true separation from your competition."

— **Joe Calloway,**
best-selling author of *A Category of One*
and member of the Professional
Speakers Hall of Fame

"We no longer have the choice to stay the same. Our world demands that we generate new solutions...*now*! Scott McKain shows us how to grow our way out of this challenging economy. Read this book NOW—you cannot afford to wait any longer."

— **Jim Cathcart,**
author of *Relationship Selling* and
recipient of Toastmaster International's
"Golden Gavel" award

"Learn how to differentiate in a way that allows you to not only survive, but thrive, in uncertain times. Don't just buy this book; *devour* it, and use it to invent your future now!"

— **Terry Paulson, PhD,**
consultant on change, and author of
Leadership Truths: One Story at a Time

"The good news about *Collapse of Distinction*? It doesn't call for big dollars—only big thinking. CEOs of organizations large and small can get excited about his plan for real distinction in the marketplace. This book is bound to put passion back in your people, projects, and customers."

— **Dianna Booher,**
Author of *The Voice of Authority: 10 Communication Strategies Every Leader Needs to Know*

"*Collapse of Distinction* clearly shows you practical, powerful, profitable steps to create a competitive advantage so you can out-market, out-sell and out-service your competition."

— **Dr. Tony Alessandra,**
author of *Collaborative Selling* and *The NEW Art of Managing People*

"*Collapse of Distinction* is another masterpiece from the brilliant business mind of Scott McKain. The lessons we learn from his unique perspective can be adapted to any business of any size."

— **Patricia Fripp, CSP, CPAE;** former president of the National Speakers Association

"For thirty-one years as an NFL referee, every time I walked off the field I asked myself if I had left the game better today than I had found it. My intention was to discover ways I could distinguish my performance—not only from others, but also from my previous efforts. *Collapse of Distinction* by Scott McKain tells what it takes to be the best you can be, whether you are running a business or refereeing a Super Bowl. I have never read a book that explains it so well. This is a must read!"

— **Dr. Jim Tunney,**
"Dean of NFL Officials," referee of three Super Bowls, member of NFL Hall of Fame, educator, and author of *It's the Will, Not the Skill*

The Collapse
of Distinction

Stand Out and Move Up
While Your Competition Fails

Scott McKain

THOMAS NELSON
Since 1798

NASHVILLE   DALLAS   MEXICO CITY   RIO DE JANEIRO   BEIJING

Other Books by Scott McKain

ALL Business Is Show Business

What Customers REALLY Want

Published in Nashville, Tennessee, by Thomas Nelson. Thomas Nelson is a registered trademark of Thomas Nelson, Inc.

Published in association with the literary agency of Daniel Literary Group, LLC, 1701 Kingsbury Drive, Suite 100, Nashville, TN 37215

Editorial staff: Joel Miller, publisher, and Thom Chittom, editor

Page design: Walter Petrie

Thomas Nelson, Inc., titles may be purchased in bulk for educational, business, fund-raising, or sales promotional use. For information, please e-mail SpecialMarkets@ThomasNelson.com.

Unless otherwise noted, Scripture quotations are taken from the King James Version.

Library of Congress Cataloging-in-Publication Data

978-1-5955-5185-6

Printed in the United States of America
08 09 10 11 12 QW 6 5 4 3 2 1

I am grateful to so many for so much—my wife, Tammy, who loves me; my stepsons, Corbin and Faron, who enlarge my capacity for life; my sister, Shelley, who motivates me; and all my friends who, I hope, enjoy time with me (and I know it's vice versa)—yet it was extraordinarily difficult to select just one to whom I should dedicate this book.

Until—the blinding flash of the obvious—I realized that without the inspiration, insight, and involvement of my father, absolutely none of what I appreciate so much about my life would have been possible.

For my dad . . .
Dallas M. McKain
June 9, 1929–August 1, 2004

Continue to Create Distinction

Our goal is to serve as a resource for you in creating the kind of compelling distinction that will continually enhance the results of your business.

We have created a special Web site to give you the opportunity to obtain the most recent, cutting-edge information, download seminars and podcasts, and share your success stories as you build distinction for your career and your organization.

Simply direct your Internet browser to http://createdistinction. com and keep your book handy. You will be asked to enter information from it for entry into a special "readers only" section.

Contents

x   Contents

Introduction

You have seen my hometown.

Just like Rock and Roll Hall of Fame member John Mellencamp, I too was "born in a small town." In fact, my birthplace is the *same* rural town of which he sings. While we both claim Seymour, Indiana for our origins, I grew up and went to school a few miles farther south in the even smaller Crothersville, Indiana—and both communities were featured in the rock star's classic music videos. I love going back to my hometown where my mother, my sister, and even my ninety-seven-year-old grandmother still live!

An old-timer in my community recently made an interesting

observation. "Scott," he said as we reminisced, "it used to be that there were two restaurants here in Crothersville. Not only did the food taste different at Ted's Restaurant than it did at Kern's Grill, but they just plain *felt* different. Each was a reflection of the owner's personality."

I nodded in agreement. Ted's was the spot where we always went after a ball game, we took a date for a burger and fries, or we simply hung out. Kern's Grill was the place where the men of the community gathered for breakfast each morning back in the late 1960s and 1970s. During the lunch break at school, I sprinted there so I could join either Mom or Dad for a quick meal. (But *never* both of them at the same time. We owned the grocery store across the street, and one of my parents always had to stay to run our family business.)

For Ted Zollman, his restaurant was his stage, and we customers were his audience. His smile was as bright as his apron. His flashing blue eyes and easy charisma were as much a part of eating there as the cheeseburgers.

On the other hand, Ted's local competitor, Alvie Kern, would sit in a booth or gruffly stand like a statue behind the counter, often with arms tightly crossed, seldom engaging in ongoing conversation. He was an observer, while his wife and daughter took care of the tables and customers.

Kern's Grill was efficient, a great place to grab a meal and go. Before you could exit the door, the white sack in which they had placed your order would display small, and growing, circles of grease. (It was a simpler time before we all knew our HDL and

LDL numbers.) Ted's Restaurant, however, was where you would order a cherry Coke, sit down, and relax, either because a friend was with you or because you knew that sooner or later, one was bound to come in and stay a while.

My old-timer friend continued, "Anymore, our fast food is the same as the fast food up the road. The McDonald's in Seymour is the same as the McDonald's in Scottsburg. In fact, they're *all* the same from Portland, Oregon, to Portland, Maine. I guess consistency is a good thing, but haven't we reached the point where we've gone overboard?

"The Wal-Mart where we shop is the same as everywhere else . . . and that's pretty much the same as K-Mart and Target. And they all sell the same items anyway. How many places do you *really* need to be able to go buy your Tide?"

He was on a roll: "My insurance agent sells the same stuff as yours, no matter what companies they work for. One has some screaming duck to represent it—another some caveman or lizard. I'm 'in good hands' one place, another is 'on my side,' while another is 'like a good neighbor.' But the problem is, I can't tell one from the next. I know the difference on my street between one of my neighbors and another. So how do I know why one *company* is a better neighbor or 'on my side' more than the other?"

Great questions.

Can your customers tell the difference between you and your competition?

If you have any professional responsibilities whatsoever—from the CEO of a Fortune 500 company to a small business entrepreneur, from someone at the home office sprinting up the corporate ladder to a salesperson slogging it out in the trenches—this question should keep you tossing and turning at night: How can *your* customers distinguish *you* from your competition?

The criterion by which this senior citizen made his determination should terrify you. It should frighten all of us who are trying to grow our businesses and our careers.

"It's just price, I guess!" he deduced. "I sure don't notice any difference between them with service. And I don't know enough about insurance, for example, to really understand the differences between their products. These days, every tree in the forest seems to be exactly alike. It's not just bland," he said. "It's *all* become the *same!*"

A Cultural Phenomenon of Epic Proportions

This wise older gentleman was not merely sharing insights regarding his perceptions about the nature of retailing. I believe he was attempting to describe what is becoming a cultural phenomenon as well as a corporate and professional nightmare: *the collapse of distinction.*

There was a time not too long ago when Chevy owners felt superior to those poor souls driving Fords and vice versa. People gained identification through the goods that they purchased, the stores where they shopped, the institutions where they invested—

no matter the level of price or sophistication of the product. But that is changing.

Over the past several years, we have seen the homogenization of practically everything. The car that I drive probably looks a lot like yours, no matter the nameplate. The big store where I shop almost certainly appears and feels a lot like yours, no matter the logo on the door, no matter the community where it's located. It looks, acts, feels the same—and it is causing a customer revolt!

In a front-page article, the *Wall Street Journal* proclaimed, "The Wal-Mart era . . . is drawing to a close." In other words, we are at the initial stages where the "faster . . . cheaper . . . perfect" generation of customers is now looking for something else—and something profoundly more difficult to deliver—from businesses. People are craving, even *coveting*, distinction!

Being different, standing out, getting noticed in a sea of sameness is vital to an organization's sustained growth and profitability. Authors J. A. Pearce and J. B. Robinson agreed in their highly regarded book, *Strategic Management*, saying that businesses that stand out "provide a service of *perceived higher value* to buyers."[1]

A Principle of Expanding Importance

When customers perceive that times are tight, they naturally want to spend their money where they receive the highest degree of value. This is the trend we are seeing today. Now is the time to stand out. And, when you do, when you highlight your business and yourself, you will find that even an economic downturn is tailor-made for grabbing market share from your competitors.

> By understanding the collapse of distinction and implementing strategies to highlight yourself and your organization, you can carve greater space between you and your competition.

It would be difficult to find any professional leader, from CEO to sales consultant, who would vote *against* standing out and looking better than the competition. Everyone is in favor of it, yet few know how to go about making distinction into reality.

The fact is that few organizations really change; instead, they merely *shuffle*. They reorganize, add managers, subtract staff, outsource, relocate offices, put more people in the field, enhance support from the corporate headquarters—all in the hopes of engineering advantages they trust will distance themselves from their competition. Such activities, however, rarely create the elements necessary to inspire distinction.

A Passion for Distinction

If you approach today's marketplace with a tepid, modest, moderate approach to gaining distinction in your field of endeavor, you had better start getting ready. Unless you become vibrant and committed to making your efforts distinct, then your customers will move on.

If you cannot find it within yourself to become emotional, committed, engaged, and yes, fervent about differentiation, then you had better be prepared to take your place among that vast throng of the mediocre who are judged by their customers solely on the basis of price. It is the singularly worst place to be in all of business. If you aren't willing to create distinction for yourself in your profession—and for your organization in the marketplace— then prepare to take your seat in the back, with the substantial swarm of the similar, where tedium reigns supreme.

If this seems a bit dramatic, just drive down the main street of most rural or suburban towns and see the deserted storefronts that once housed businesses of all types. They now sit silently as monuments to the deaths of organizations that have become casualties of the collapse of distinction.

But don't worry.

You hold in your hands a simple, practical road map to understand why—seemingly all of a sudden—everything seems so much the same. In addition, this book should serve as a guide to assist you in making your organization distinct from the competitors in your industry. To craft this information, I consulted with and lectured to some of the nation's most dynamic organizations. In addition, I have had a role in creating and building a business generating more than $100 million in annual revenues from nineteen different companies in highly diverse industries. However, my primary goal here is not to promote my business, but to be the catalyst that causes you to think—and think deeply—about *yours!*

What's in Store for You?

You already know you have to stand out to get noticed. My job is to help you do just that. To accomplish our mission, I'll present some background into how this collapse of distinction came about in the marketplace, because no great changes ever happen without some degree of historical perspective. I'll then briefly illustrate what has been the typical approach of most organizations, regardless of their size or products. (These traditional steps have, for the most part, failed miserably.) Finally, I'll give you several basic, yet specific, ideas regarding how you can develop tactics that will make you and your organization distinct.

Meeting the baseline expectations of your customers is not enough. Therefore, I will provide for you, at the conclusion of this journey toward distinction, several additional resources that are immediately available and constantly updated. I hope *The Collapse of Distinction* will make a valuable contribution to your organization and your career—as well as provide an experience of the very attribute we are examining.

Executive Summary

At the conclusion of each chapter, you'll find a short "executive summary" of the major points of that particular installment. The goal of the review is not to give you just a quick, one-paragraph re-hash, but instead a more intensive compendium enabling you to review the material with just a quick skim. In addition, this summary can become your "talking points" as you describe the material to your colleagues.

I. Everything seems the same

    a. As the "old-timer" in my hometown pointed out, the points of differentiation between businesses in our community and others across the nation have been practically eliminated.

    b. This phenomenon makes it significantly more difficult for your customers to be able to distinguish a difference between you and your competitors in the market place.

II. This challenge is expanding in significance

    a. All it takes is a trip down the main street of almost every mid-sized town to see closed storefronts of businesses that failed to distinguish themselves in the market.

    b. If your customers cannot differentiate you, then they will fall back upon the one point where they can always discover a distinction—*price*.

    c. Price is the single worst point of differentiation for any organization in any industry.

      i. It leads to lower margins; which, in turn, leads to fewer resources for developing our people or enhancing our products.

III. Distinction requires passion

  a. Most organizations do not change. They merely *shuffle*.

      i. They reorganize, add or change management, subtract staff, outsource, relocate, and more—all in the hopes of stumbling onto something that will reconnect them with customers.

      ii. Few of these efforts create the elements necessary to inspire distinction.

  b. If you cannot create passion within yourself and your organization to create distinction for your business—and differentiation from your competition—you are doomed to mediocrity in today's changing and highly challenging market.

IV. The goal of this book

  a. The main objectives of *The Collapse of Distinction* are to:

      i. Provide a roadmap for understanding how this phenomenon of "sameness" happened—and what you can do about it.

      ii. Be a guide to assist you in making your business—and yourself—distinct in the marketplace.

iii. Outline strategies you can execute to make a difference that endears you to customers—and makes you enduring as an organization and professional.

Action Steps, Questions, and Ideas

At the end of each chapter there are a few questions and action steps for you as you complete your journal or notebook and prepare to attack the collapse of distinction.

- Make a list of the ways that you believe your customers can tell the difference between you and your competition.

- Other than product and price—what do you really sell? Make a list.

- Why would a customer pay for yours over and above your competition's? Develop three reasons.

- What is your level of commitment to achieving organizational and individual distinction?

One
How Did We Get in This Mess?

The moment was one of the most surreal that I have ever experienced. I was a farm kid from Crothersville, Indiana, part of a team invited by the international organization People to People on a goodwill mission. At home, the United States was in the midst of a presidential election between our only nonelected president and a peanut farmer from Georgia. It was our bicentennial year. But that day I was standing in Red Square, in Moscow, in the Soviet Union—at the very center of communism.

Even though it was September, the day was unseasonably cold and gray. Behind my colleagues and me was the bland and massive GUM Department Store, occupying a significant space on Red Square. In front of us was the tomb of the father of communism, his body resting inside appearing almost as a wax figure. Just beyond that loomed the sight of the imposing Kremlin. The sentries at Lenin's Tomb goose-stepped their way through the changing of the guard in a manner that I had witnessed only in old black-and-white newsreel footage of the Nazi soldiers from Hitler's Germany. Their precision and efficiency were completely devoid of emotion.

As the ceremony silently concluded, a short, rotund senior citizen stopped me and asked in broken English if I was, in fact, an American. I affirmatively answered with pride for my country yet with a bit of fear. He opened his coat and pointed to a scar on his chest. With tears in his eyes, he gestured at his wound and said, "From war. *Please*. No war. No more war."

Wait, We're the Good Guys!

I was stunned. Like most Americans of that era, I assumed that the *Soviets* were the aggressors, not us! Nevertheless, here was an obviously earnest Russian who firmly believed that *we* were the enemy. Slowly I assured him that war was *not* our intent, and I hoped it wasn't the objective of his country either. I emphasized that my colleagues and I were greatly enjoying our visit and were grateful to see his homeland. As someone standing beside him translated my English into his Russian, he broke into a wide, toothy smile and nodded rapidly in agreement.

I then asked him, "How could you pick me out of this large crowd as being an American?"

He spoke to his friend, who then turned to me and said, "Your clothes have color. You are smiling, having fun, as you are in Red Square. That gave it all away." The fact that my clothes were not the standard-issue Soviet-gray, and the fact that I seemed to be enjoying myself, set me apart from the crowd. It pegged me as someone from another place. It was a lesson in being *different*— the lesson of this book.

What I saw in the Soviet Union of the seventies was the result of conformity and similarity, typical of what happens when the state owns or controls almost everything. The emphasis on uniformity seems to be a constant of every monolithic institution. But communism isn't the only thing that produces it. Ironically enough, competition serves just as well.

The Three Destroyers of Differentiation

This chapter focuses on the three destroyers that created the collapse of distinction. Taken individually, each of these destroyers creates a compelling challenge for you in the marketplace. When combined, they have a synergistic and destructive impact on your industry, your organization, and you.

Differentiation Destroyer #1: Capitalism Produces Incremental Advancement

Our first destroyer means that in our competitive capitalistic society, the bar is continually going to be raised. We will constantly seek advantages for our products and services that move customers to choose us over the other guys and gals. When you are faced with a competitive situation, you've got to constantly get *better,* and provide *more compelling* reasons for your customers to spend money with you—or you will go out of business.

But here's the rub. When my competitor creates a point of differentiation, my natural inclination is to either merely imitate the improvement, or to attempt to *incrementally* improve upon the advancement. If you get ahead of me with a new advancement or strategy, my natural response is to *replicate* it. If I merely duplicate your effort, it is easy for my customer base—and my colleagues within my organization—to perceive that you no longer have a competitive advantage.

However, if your new method has enabled you to gain significant traction in the marketplace, then my best move appears to be to attempt to imitate whatever created your advantage, and attempt to marginally do you one better.

Notice the problem: in both examples, my efforts are based upon what my *competitor* is doing, not what my *customers* desire. And in most cases, such advancements are evolutionary—not revolutionary. I am probably thinking that I don't want to stick my neck out too far because you may chop it off in front of our customers and prospects. (Since we are competitors, *my* customers are *your* prospects and vice versa.) You feel the same way. The result is incremental, uninspiring advancement that appears to be safe. Instead, however, we mutually destroy any points of differentiation that can better serve our customers and enhance our respective organizations.

The perfect model of capitalism is that you and I compete *for the customer*. Our competitive efforts reduce costs—and, therefore, the price of our goods and services—while each of us also brings innovation to the marketplace so that it benefits the client. We continue to strive to meet the client's needs while, at the same time, we grow our respective organizations through the enhanced business we are achieving through the superior value we are providing.

Yet in almost every case in the real world, we instead compete *against each other*. Our focus seems to be directed toward others in the same industry that produce a similar product and deliver similar services, all the while playing the internal political games inherent within any organization.

When Times Become Difficult

Add the element of a challenging economic forecast, and it seems to enhance our desire to play "follow the leader" with our competition. They cut staff; we do too. They close a location; we do too.

All of us pull in our horns, hunker down, and attempt to ride out the busts. It is overwhelming how many companies focus on not losing to the competition rather than on delivering what customers really want.

If you follow sports to any great degree, you are familiar with the stories of the teams that lost important games because they played not to lose. By going into the "prevent defense" too early in football or by slowing down the game and holding onto the ball in basketball, stellar teams have gotten out of the flow of the game and become so tense that they lost the ability to execute at their normal, highly skilled level of play.

Tennis professional and instructor Ron Waite makes an important distinction when discussing this phenomenon with his students. He tells them that playing "cautiously" is not the same as playing "smartly."[1] The same thing is almost always true in business. When we direct our focus cautiously toward the competition, we seldom execute the smart strategy for winning and keeping customers.

Customers Raise Their Expectations

Customers also play a part in enforcing this kind of incremental advance. They too participate in the first destroyer of differentiation. It is part of the DNA, if you will, of our system that the competitive, capitalistic form of economics will also goad customers into steadily, methodically increasing their demands, no

matter the economic climate. The best explanation of why consumers do this comes from a close friend of mine, Dr. Michael
LeBoeuf, the best-selling author of one of my favorite business
books, *GMP: The Greatest Management Principle in the World*.[2] His
principle is simply this: "Behavior rewarded is behavior repeated."
Consider for a moment how that principle comes into play with
regard to customer demands.

> **Behavior rewarded is behavior
> repeated, especially when it comes
> to escalating customer demands.**

Here's an example from the automotive industry: if I work
until five o'clock and your service department closes at the same
time, we both have a problem. I can't get my car serviced, and
you can't get my business. But if your dealership responds to
my situation by staying open additional hours, I am going to
reward you with my business. Behavior rewarded is behavior
repeated. That is the first outcome, and it explains why businesses
that get rewarded for superior customer service—for example,
Nordstrom, Southwest Airlines, and Starbucks, to state a few of
the obvious—become even *more* focused on strategies that connect them with their customers.

The second outcome is less obvious. Because you have rewarded
my demands as a customer in a manner that I recognize to be positive (I need extended hours for service, and you've accommodated

my request), I will now intuitively feel compelled to make *additional* demands. You seem to prize my behavior; therefore, I—and the multitude of customers just like me—will repeat it.

No Good Deed Goes Unpunished

Why don't I, your customer, just relax, content in my appreciation for a service bay that remains open until midnight? Because you have rewarded my request—behavior rewarded is behavior repeated. I'm going to replicate and enhance my expectations. What *else* can you do for me?

> Doing good means your
> customers will hasten their
> demand for you to do better!

Am I suggesting that you stop acquiescing to customer requests and demands? Of course not. But you need to understand two important points:

1. Customer demands are always going to accelerate.
2. This phenomenon is true for you—and your competition.

Therefore—since we are all confronted with a customer base accelerating its demands—if your competition finds you have a point of competitive advantage, especially one that is perceived to be ongoing and sustainable—it is inherent in our system for them to try to improve their product or service (as mentioned earlier), imitate your advantage (also previously stated), or *cut their price* to reduce your superior positioning.

A Dangerous Outcome

What occurs when neither you nor I can think of much more we can do to improve our product or service? What ensues when you have already imitated me as much as you can, and I have already done the same to you? Here's what happens:

1. You cut your price to develop some point of advantage.

2. I do the same to keep up with your discounting.

3. We both erode our profit margins, which means there are fewer resources for either of us to innovate and distinguish our efforts.

4. We corrode any distinction—and the related goodwill and loyalty—that customers perceive about our organization's products and services, which leads to the potential spiral of price pressures, which further diminishes any possibility that we break the cycle.

As simple as this sounds, I often deal with some company, management team, or sales force in assorted industries that wakes up to discover it is on this treadmill with very little perspective on how it got there—and no strategy for how to extricate itself. And that's just the *initial* one of the three destroyers. Combine the impact of this first point with the next one:

Differentiation Destroyer #2: Dynamic Change Is Delivering New Competition

If you have not already read it, please allow me to recommend a highly compelling book: Eric Schlosser's *Fast Food Nation*.[3] After you digest his material, I'll wager you won't consume a hamburger for weeks! You may not agree with all of the points that Schlosser advocates, but I'll bet you cannot put his book aside.

While most of Schlosser's work does for the fast-food industry what Upton Sinclair did decades earlier for meatpacking, I find it highly interesting to view the early part of the book as a real historical examination of what transpired in our country from a *cultural*—as opposed to dietary or culinary—perspective. He outlines how fast-food franchises exploded on the back of the interstate highway system. Distribution got easier, and so did copycat capitalism. Businesses of every type, from department stores and electronics mega-centers to specialty coffee shops, multiplied in a frenzy of duplication and imitation. Schlosser traces the steps that ensured our nation would experience the collapse of distinction.

Taking the Adventure out of Lunch

"In my day," my dad would brag, "stopping for lunch was an adventure." He did not mean that as a positive point! He meant that as you traveled down a two-lane state or U.S. highway, you'd keep an eye out for a diner where the truckers were eating. Believe it or not, the common belief at the time was that the truckers— who were eating exponentially more meals on the road than the average American traveler—would naturally know where the best places were to dine.

As the son and grandson of truck drivers, I must respectfully assert that I have absolutely no idea how our collective thinking became so twisted that those who hauled interstate commerce also became our pseudo-reliable source of gastronomic expertise. Nonetheless, without a doubt, that was the thinking prior to the arrival and rapid expansion of the interstate system.

However, when the dual-lane, rapid-transit superhighways opened, those pioneer travelers whisking down the Interstate soon discovered that they no longer had to endure the mysteries of Main Street U.S.A. Instead, the new generation of fast-driving travelers wanted to jump off an exit, fill up their tanks, and dine quickly.

I can still recall Dad's unique delight at the fact that every McDonald's was almost exactly identical. A Big Mac tasted the same no matter where you bought it. He quickly purchased that coronary-on-a-sesame-seed-bun, ensured his kids remained relatively quiet and happy with their meals, and kept the pedal to the metal. No one in the cramped Chevy dared to complain about the meal because it was the very same lunch everyone had eaten and liked just fine yesterday, four hundred miles back up the road.

As conventional wisdom and Schlosser suggest, the smaller chains that were simultaneously developing and expanding did not have the wealth of capital on hand to execute the extensive site-selection procedures that became so scientific and strategic at McDonald's Corporation. So these competitors did the next best thing: they bought property as close to a McDonald's as possible. Instead of McDonald's having a monopoly on interstate highway exchanges, the corporation inadvertently pioneered a boom of investments in farmland plots slightly away from the Main Street commercial areas of the vast number of communities adjoining the interstate highway.

Seemingly in the blink of an eye, Alvie Kern of Crothersville—and thousands of small business owners just like him—was in serious economic trouble for the first time in his entrepreneurial life. He was confronted with competition he had never imagined in his wildest dreams. He was facing rivals that barely existed, as far as he knew, just a few years earlier.

Put yourself in Alvie's shoes for a moment. You are not a businessperson, no matter what your hometown believes. You are a *sandwich person*. You've always known how to make a great blue plate special, and that has always served you and your customers very well. Now, however, your patrons can drive through a fast-food chain restaurant four miles down the road from you and still be back at work before you can get them and their greasy white bags of food out your front door. I still remember Alvie constantly grousing in his cigarette-induced, gravelly voice that he didn't understand how "anyone could eat that McDonald's junk"—all the while losing business to the chain in droves. How do you compete? What do you do?

The Fatal Approach of the Non-differentiated

If you were like most people in that or a similar situation, your reaction to Destroyer #2—dynamic cultural, technological, and societal change delivering new competitors to your doorstep—is to execute precisely the *wrong* strategy. If you are a small-town diner-owner like Alvie, you will erroneously tend to believe that your product is a hamburger. If you build the better burger, you assume that you will become the better burger business once again. Many of your customers are now going to McDonald's, so you try to "out-McDonald's" the competition and restore your hometown business. Unfortunately, despite your best intentions, you cannot out-original the initial player in almost every situation.

Fast-food chains proliferated—but why? The key to their success was to build on McDonald's efforts at consistency, but find *specific points of differentiation* that enabled them to obtain their unique place in the market. Therefore, flame-broiled and 100 percent fresh (not frozen) beef, roast beef sandwiches, or tacos rather than burgers, succeeded—while the outmatched local diner often did not.

"But wait a minute," you may be thinking. "Your hometown establishment *did* have points of differentiation. It had a local, engaged proprietor who poured his—and his family's—heart and soul into the business. You've already pointed out that it had a unique taste and atmosphere. Wasn't that enough?"

No. And the reason why leads us to Destroyer #3:

Differentiation Destroyer #3: Familiarity Breeds Complacency

One thing I heard often from my mom was "familiarity breeds contempt." As much as I hate to dispute my mother's advice, my experience has taught me that this one isn't true. If you become more familiar with someone, it does not automatically guarantee that you will become contemptuous of him or her.

When something like a product or service is present so much that it becomes thoroughly familiar and is boundlessly available, we do not then begin to scorn it, hate it, or express disdain toward it. Instead, we begin to take it for granted. We become *complacent* and presume it will always be around.

We see this all the time in our private lives. We, unfortunately, take for granted the people who are closest to us. We don't intend disrespect toward our spouses, for example. It just seems to be a part of the human makeup. We presuppose that if something or someone is overwhelmingly familiar, it represents a garden we no longer need to tend as enthusiastically or systematically. We erroneously assume that the love will always be there on the vine, and it doesn't require as much nurturing, intensity, or the commitment of time that is demanded by something that we have yet to acquire.

Taking It for Granted

That was a significant problem for Kern's Grill. We always went there for lunch, so we took it for granted. To try someplace new—like McDonald's then, and perhaps your competitor now—was fun, different, and therefore exciting! It honestly never occurred to us that because the members of our family went to McDonald's a few times a week instead of Kern's Grill, Alvie's business would be so severely affected. But it was.

The reason is obvious. Just as we felt our slight shift in patronage would not cause a seismic economic change in the grill's fortunes, neither did others in town believe they possessed so much clout. However, when a portion of the McKains' business at Kern's Grill—as well as the business of just about every other family like us in town—was subtracted, a *significant* portion of the revenues of one little family diner was erased. It never crossed our minds that we were murdering a business, and we even owned a small establishment across the street.

This phenomenon of business psychology has fascinated me

for years. Business owners do not think like business owners when they are customers someplace else. They think like customers. Salespeople do not think like salespeople when they are shopping. They think like customers. When a corporate CEO purchases a trailer to haul his collector-grade automobile from us at Obsidian, he doesn't think like a CEO. He thinks like a customer. When we are customers, we all assume the customer position.

Conversely, the same is often true in the attitude of a business toward its loyal customers. For reasons that I believe are impossible to rationalize once they are discovered, we tend to pursue new customers with more enthusiasm than we prize existing ones. As I wrote in *What Customers REALLY Want*, every organization or professional on the planet has some kind of acquisition strategy—in other words, a specific plan for attracting new customers. However, few companies or professionals have a *retention* strategy, a precise program that outlines specific steps to keep current customers and grow the business we are obtaining from them.[4]

Once again, the example of our personal lives is the perfect metaphor for customer retention and growth. Every marriage counselor will tell you that one way to grow a relationship is to continue to romance the person who has already committed his or her life to you. When we are dating, we do all of the steps necessary to grow the relationship. We make phone calls and send flowers, cards, or e-mails. We try to surprise our loved one with little efforts that are out of the ordinary and above and beyond normal dating. Unfortunately, it all ends at "I do" for many couples.

Why is that true? I honestly don't know, and I'm not really qualified to speculate. Business philosopher Jim Rohn simply calls it, "One of the mysteries of the mind." That is just the way most people are. He advises that rather than excessively ponder and attempt to discover the reasons for this behavioral abnormality at length, we should instead do something more productive—such as challenge ourselves to be better than the crowd.[5]

What Did Kern's Grill Do?

Had Kern's Grill been more customer-focused prior to the advent of drive-through fast food, then perhaps the diner could have survived the McDonald's onslaught. But because it wasn't truly differentiated and the owners took their customers for granted, then lamely tried to imitate the hot new competitors, they were caught in the collapse of distinction.

Kern's Grill died a relatively short death in Crothersville. Alvie Kern just didn't have the capital to make the strategic business investments that might have created the differentiation needed to survive. Frankly, he probably did not possess the business acumen to do so, even if he had the cash. As I recall, he basically stated that he was closing the restaurant for "health reasons." As my dad said—with more than a slight bit of fear regarding how quickly fortunes could change for business owners in the face of new competition—the health problem was probably the fact that losing his business was killing him.

WIIFU—What's in It for Us?

What does the demise of a greasy spoon diner in a small town have to do with your organization? Well, *everything*.

Think it happens only to insignificant businesses in undersized markets? Think again!

Consider the world of retailing—not just in a solitary small town, but also throughout America. Then, picture yourself as Montgomery Ward.

Aaron Montgomery Ward created perhaps the initial mail-order corporation in 1872, with an innovative single-sheet catalog offering 163 items. Additionally, he earned recognition as the first national retailer in the United States to create a "satisfaction guaranteed" offer to his customers.[6] This superior service and an impressive assortment of quality goods at affordable prices led to rapid growth.

What do you imagine Montgomery Ward thought about when, back in 1886, fourteen years after Ward's founding, Richard W. Sears started a business in Minneapolis selling watches to fellow train stationmasters with his company that was first known as the R. W. Sears Watch Company? My guess is that Mr. Sears wasn't even on the radar screen (especially since radar screens weren't invented until many decades later).

Continue your rapid progression through mass-market retail history to the time a small business in Bentonville, Arkansas, entered the same fray. Do you believe that Sears even gave this upstart a second thought at that point? "Come on," you can imagine them saying in the halls of their extravagant corporate headquarters, "their leader is a hick named Walton who drives a pickup! We cannot imagine that his company is going to be a player on our field."

And if you are sitting now in the midst of that Arkansas empire, I suggest that you should be wondering what you must figure out to prevent this Destroyer of Differentiation from doing to your organization what Sears did to Wards—and you did to Sears. If you are Microsoft, you're worried about Google. Sony has to just hate Apple's iPod for what it did to the Walkman.

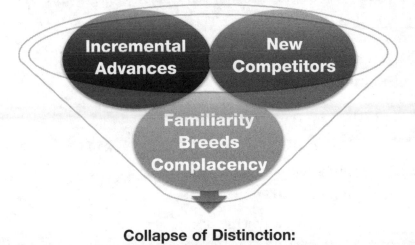

Collapse of Distinction:
The Three Destroyers of Differentiation.

The cycle continues on and on.

I hope you realize that differentiating your business is imperative, not just to create space in today's marketplace from the competitors you are already encountering everyday. It's also vital because there are going to be new contestants for your customers of whom you are not yet aware.

Consider this amalgamation of challenges: the constantly elevating demands of customers, a tightening economy, and more competitors than ever—that are easier for prospects to access. How could you possibly consider doing business in today's economic and competitive climate *without* being differentiated? Establishing distinction in your market—and starting now—is vital in creating the future you want for your organization in today's hypercompetitive global economy.

The great news is that you can employ strategies that will build distinction immediately. This book will show you how.

Executive Summary

I. There are Three Destroyers of Differentiation

    a. Each of these Destroyers have had a powerful impact upon organizations—and individual careers—in the marketplace.

    b. However, the synergistic impact when viewed collectively is much more significant—and important—to you and your organization.

II. Differentiation Destroyer #1: Incremental Advancement

    a. Our capitalistic system ideally should produce a competitive situation where we have to:

        i. Continually improve; and,

        ii. Provide more compelling reasons for customers to do business with us.

        iii. Because, our competition will, theoretically, be doing the same thing.

    b. In the real world, however, we have been doing something different.

        i. If my competition creates a point of differentiation, my natural tendency is to:

            1. *Imitate* or even *replicate* your advancement

            2. *Incrementally* improve upon your advancement

    c. Notice the inherent problem here: By focusing upon what the competitor is doing, it also means that our activity is centered upon the competition rather than the customer!

        i. We are competing *against each other*—rather than *for the customer.*

    d. In addition, this also essentially means that we are executing *evolutionary* advancements—rather than the *revolutionary* ones that true differentiation requires.

e. When economic times become more challenging, we also tend to all pull in our horns and ride out the recession.

   i. This usually means we provide even *less* of what our customers really want—even as our competition does exactly the same thing we are doing.

   ii. The result is dissatisfied customers—who decide they can spend less with all of us.

   1. In part, because they cannot tell the difference between any of us!

III. Differentiation Destroyer #2: Dynamic New Competition

a. In a former time, the then-new Interstate Highway System provided a new and faster connection between communities.

   i. However, a residual impact was that it also accelerated the speed of growth of fast-food restaurants and chain retailers.

   ii. As these new businesses appeared, entrenched local retailers were confronted with new competition they barely knew existed a short time earlier.

b. The existing retailers often executed precisely the *wrong* strategy:

    i. Often they attempted to replicate the perceived advantages of the dynamic new competitor.

       1. Note that, given Destroyer #1, this response is easy to predict.

    ii. They usually discovered that if their competition was McDonald's, for example, they could not "out-McDonald's" the original.

       1. Only through the development of specific points of differentiation could a business establish a unique place in the market.

       2. Many retailers—steeped primarily in product knowledge, and possessing a smaller degree of marketing and finance acumen—were not up to this challenging task.

c. In most cases, customers chose the new—and differentiated—option.

    i. Which, of course, often resulted in the demise of the non-differentiated competitor.

IV. Differentiation Destroyer #3: Familiarity Breeds Complacency

a. It's not what we were told as kids—familiarity does not breed "contempt"

    i. When we have become familiar with something—and it is boundlessly available—we do not scorn it, hate it, or hold it in contempt.

ii. Instead, we take it for granted.

b. When we take something for granted, we no longer play as active a part in its growth and cultivation.

i. When that happens in regards to a personal and professional relationship, it often means that the association dies for lack of attention.

ii. When that impact is multiplied for a business across a wide range of customers, the result can be fatal for the company.

V. The impact of these Destroyers can be felt in every organization

a. While the metaphor of the book is a small town diner, the fact is that practically every organization is suffering from the synergistic impact of these Three Destroyers of Differentiation.

b. The fundamental question here is simply: How in the world could you possibly consider facing today's challenging economic climate without striving to attain differentiation?

c. The goal of this book is to show you how it is done.

Action Steps, Questions, and Ideas

- How have you imitated your competitors? How have they copied you? Develop a list.

- What new competition has technology delivered to your doorstep? What is your strategy to combat it?

- Where are your customers most familiar with your organization? Are they so familiar that they have become bored?

Two

Why Don't I Like My Work Anymore?

"Why is it so much easier to lay off factory workers than any other employees?" a manager rhetorically asked me with a smirk.

I shook my head—in part because I didn't know the answer he was seeking, and in part because I couldn't believe he would ask such an insensitive question.

"Because," the manager continued, "there are just so darn many of them, and they are all so much alike."

Stunned at his crassness, I had to admit that he was correct nevertheless. A company can eradicate elements that are indistinguishable much easier than it can cut a component that generates a recognizable difference. If an employee in Bangalore can produce a product or service that is no different from one made or performed in Baltimore, why wouldn't an organization seeking to maximize profitability go with the least expensive alternative?

> No matter your occupation, you are threatened by the impact of the collapse of distinction.

While we can understand the organization's decision from the standpoint of a "case study," it is one heck of a lot different when the job eliminated is *ours*! When the challenges and pressures brought upon organizations from the phenomenon we are discussing creates personal impact, it accelerates our need for understanding. This chapter will change our focus from the effect of this phenomenon on organizations, and begin to examine the insidious influence of the Three Destroyers on your career . . . and you!

Let's Examine Examples

To illustrate these challenges, let's pick a couple of areas of concentration, understanding that these are merely metaphors for the peril in which we *all* find ourselves.

Let's assume that you are a financial advisor. You care about your clients and their goals and dreams. Nevertheless, just when you thought that your business was going to start becoming a little bit easier—since your ongoing tenure should mean a continually larger and growing book of business—it seems that someone changed all the rules. You cannot figure out what happened. You went to periodic seminars and improved your business and yourself a little bit every single year. Yet clients now seem bored or distracted when you bring them in for their annual reviews. And when you are home on a Sunday afternoon watching your favorite NFL team, you can't help getting a little edgy at the parade of commercials for E*Trade, Charles Schwab, Scottrade, and other online brokers.

Your firm compensates you, in part, for obtaining new assets to manage and for the acquisition of new households of affluent investors for the firm. But both are becoming harder to attain, not just because these new competitors attract prospects away from you or because of volatility in the market. It's also because you are having a more difficult time *keeping your current clients* in the fold.

And the impact isn't solely professional. It has become so much more difficult that you aren't having fun anymore. The dramatic financial events of recent times may mean the firm where you work has been acquired by a competitor or is in danger of collapse as an institution altogether. You are always looking over your shoulder, wondering when the next client may go away. If the market goes down, you retreat into hiding, fearing that if you contact your clients, they may move their accounts elsewhere. Somewhere deep inside, you also realize that if you fail to call them, they may think you don't really care about their business and move their accounts elsewhere.

Now let's assume you are the owner of a small business, much like my parents with our grocery store—or Alvie Kern with his diner. Without realizing it, you face challenges similar to those of our financial advisor. Let's say you are working hard to own and manage the best independent dry cleaner in your mid-sized city. You've upgraded the interiors of your stores, you've become more environmentally sensitive regarding the chemicals used, and you pride yourself on the care you display to your customers' clothes.

Yet when the competitor located down the street cuts the price on shirts to $1.99, some of your customers choose him, instead. You are hurt and a bit upset. You attended the trade association meeting every year and learned the latest techniques and approaches in your industry. No one would argue with you that you are the best dry cleaner in town, but business isn't growing.

You start noticing all the advertisements for steamers at department stores. They claim that if you steam your suits and dresses, you won't have to pay to dry clean them as often. Now, all of a sudden it seems, your competition includes not only that other cleaner down the street, but mega-retailers such as Target, as well.

So, you let a couple of people go and work longer hours

yourself, trying to keep your overhead reasonable. Longtime customers ask you in a whisper if "anything's wrong," and some seldom come in. You are more tired and cranky than ever before, and you wonder whether you really should have sold insurance or real estate instead of opening a dry cleaning establishment.

The Three Destroyers are already at work undermining your business! Here's how:

Destroyer #1: Emulation

You envisioned that by keeping pace with the competition that was around you every day, your efforts would enable you to be close to the local apex of your profession. That's Destroyer #1! You always felt your competitors were the other financial advisors at your office—certainly, no more than the ones at the other local firms. Or if you are the entrepreneur, you could keep your eye on your rival because he was the other cleaner down the block. Therefore, you executed only incremental improvements, not significant ones that would create distinction.

If a competing financial advisor had a client meeting that involved a wine tasting that received positive reviews, you did exactly the same. Maybe you even stepped it up a modest amount, hired the sommelier from a good local restaurant, and had a wine tasting just a bit more sophisticated than your rival at the other financial firm. If the cleaner down the street offered same-day service, you did too. If he advertised "In by 9:00–out by 5:00," you bought a sign that stated, "In by 9:30–out by 4:30" because you believed that gave you a significant advantage.

Were you inspired to change your practice or your business in a dramatic manner? Of course not. You didn't reconstruct your client base, nor did you become innovative in what you did. Either you:

1. Emulated your competitors so that they couldn't achieve significant competitive differentiation, or

2. You delivered what you perceived to be the minimum degree of advancement required to establish yourself over your competitor as the primary provider of the goods and services inherent in your profession.

Here is the problem: *neither* strategy creates distinction.

The first—emulation—merely does enough to keep your competitors in check. It does not create space in the marketplace; *it ensures that a pack of non-differentiated competitors includes you!*

The second—a minimum degree of advancement—maintains your positioning, *but fails to create the type of distinction that inspires the passion that results in client loyalty and engagement.*

The Wisdom of . . . a Wrestler?

Ric Flair is a longtime star in professional wrestling. His real name is Richard Morgan Fliehr, and he was born in February 1949. I mention that to suggest that if someone can be almost sixty years old and still maintain significant success in his profession—by getting in the ring wearing nothing more than glorified Speedo trunks, while possessing a somewhat less-than-glorious physique, and still be cheered by thousands of adoring young fans—then maybe, just maybe, he has something to say that we should consider.

I discovered a little wisdom in his book that I noticed at a bookstore one day. It's a no-nonsense nugget of the philosophy that creates differentiation: To *be* the man . . . you gotta *beat* the man!"[1]

While Ric Flair has recently retired from the ring, he still makes an important point. Every professional I know wants to *be* the man—or the woman—who is highly successful. Yet few want to *beat* the man to achieve that goal. They want to *tie* the man or to *edge out* the man. They desire to do nothing *more* than the man. In other words, they want to execute the *least progressive, most conforming activity* they can to achieve the success they desire. They choose to walk the traditional path instead of taking Robert Frost's legendary "road not taken" to get to where they want to go in life and work. They want to triumph by a trivial margin, when true builders of distinction are never satisfied with the incremental. These distinctive players want to beat the man so soundly that the competitor is no longer even considered.

And so the question becomes: How important is it to you to be differentiated, to achieve distinction, to be the man or woman?

Destroyer #2: New Competition Means New Challenges

Guess what, you have new competition knocking (electronically or in person) on your clients' doors! And, this creates an even more difficult challenge for you because of your response to Destroyer #1.

Because you failed to create an innovative approach to the way that you deal with your clients—and because you evaluated your success against a band of bland brothers in the profession or industry—your customers have stopped seeing how your specific involvement in their financial affairs or dry cleaning is bringing any significant value to their lives. If a client doesn't feel you offer exceptional value or a compelling experience, why not make inexpensive online trades or why not steam the dress at home? Clients will always find a point of distinction. Therefore, if you fail to outline one for them in compelling fashion, they will go to the worst possible distinguisher for you: *price*.

Don't Live by the Sword

Price is no safe harbor against the constant pressure of competition. Everyone is vulnerable to it, both the innovators of yesterday and the big businesses of today, because price knows no brand. It is not loyal to a community or a company or a history. That means that price is no real friend of distinction. Discount brokerages, to continue our example, are discovering this for themselves. In *USA Today*, reporter Matt Krantz wrote,

> Upstart online brokerages, such as Zecco.com, and aggressive banks, such as Wells Fargo and Bank of America, are giving the big four online brokerages—E-Trade, TD Ameritrade, Charles Schwab and Scottrade—a run for their money, and for yours, with offers of free online trades.
>
> "There are competitive pressures on the larger players," says James Lohmann, senior director at J. D. Power, a company that rates online brokerages. "Everyone has gotten cheaper," says Kurt Feierabend, 38, a consultant in Minneapolis who has had an account with TD Ameritrade and *is looking to switch to a broker with lower fees.*[2]

Go back and reread the customer's comment. Mr. Feierabend does not indicate that he is dissatisfied in any manner with TD Ameritrade. It's just that he is looking to switch so he can pay *lower fees*. Which, of course, makes sense for him and is horrible news for TD Ameritrade.

I guess we could say, "Live by the price sword, die by the price sword." TD Ameritrade—and the other major online brokers mentioned in the article—launched their businesses with discount trading as their distinguishing characteristic over the Merrill Lynch, UBS, Morgan Stanley types of firms. Now, these

Web-based discounters find themselves confronted with the challenge of Destroyer #2.

Entrepreneurs face similar challenges. To continue our independent business example, consider what Andrea Holecek wrote in the *Munster, Indiana, Times:* "Linda Dygert, who owns Valparaiso's Mercury Cleaners with her husband, Norm, said for someone just starting in the business . . . [it] could be a nightmare. The Dygerts have owned their business since they bought it from his father in 1982." Mrs. Dygert states in the article that

> the biggest challenge is trying to be competitive and do the right thing. But I wouldn't recommend anyone getting into the business. My husband works six days a week. On the seventh day he does maintenance. He gets up at 5 [a.m. and] leaves the business at 5:30 [p.m.] when it closes. So there are very long hours and huge commitments. And you're never out of debt because you always have to buy new equipment.[3]

I'm certain the Dygerts do a terrific job. However, on a generic basis, have you done business at a place where the owner loves her job and you can tell? Have you patronized stores where you just know they're trapped and wouldn't wish their business—or lives—on anyone? Do they ever take out their frustrations on their ever-dwindling number of customers?

No matter what your field, you will experience competitive pressures. What will your response be? What will you do? Here's a tip: it had better not involve price!

Destroyer #3: Customer Boredom

Your customers are bored, and I'll bet you never saw it coming. You bring in your clients for their annual reviews, let them know that your performance beat the market average by 4 percent, fill them in on new investments you have discovered that are congruent with their preferred approaches and risk tolerances, and you can almost see their eyes glaze over! How in the world could they be bored when you are talking about something so important?

Your clients are bored because familiarity breeds complacency.

Think this is an isolated phenomenon? Hardly. As Joe Edwards reported in *Nation's Restaurant News* all the way back in 1984, Brock Hotel Corporation—parent company of a chain of restaurants—was struggling with the choices needed to solve the problems created by customer boredom. Customer boredom was "a real problem," and fighting it was critical to the success of the concept.

What was boring the customers? Believe it or not, ShowBiz Pizza! The stores consisted of twice-a-week teen dance centers with a $20,000 package (in 1984 dollars) of disco lights, dance floor, and sound equipment, as well as one-hundred-seat theaters featuring dazzling films, such as a twenty-three-minute movie with special effects created by Douglas Trumbull, the cinematic genius who worked on several major motion pictures including *Close Encounters of the Third Kind*.[4]

Now, if *that* is boring to customers, what are you doing to excite them? (And it bears mentioning that those adolescent customers in 1984 are now—a quarter century later—your adult customers.)

Customers don't call the phone company to say thanks because they have a dial tone. What is truly an amazing piece of technological delivery is taken for granted. *The Grocer* reported in its October 2005 edition, "Grocery shopping has become so boring that some consumers are more excited by the nonfood in their supermarkets, according to new IGD research." Yet grocery shopping today offers more choices, convenience, and experience than ever before!

Like it or not, customers are going to treat your efforts with similar ennui.

What have you changed in the past year in your approach to your customers?

If they know your routine almost as well as you do, then you have substantial problems. What makes *you* different?

The Trifecta!

Wow! What a combination you have going for you!

1. You are creating only incremental improvements so nothing really distinguishes you from your competition in any meaningful fashion.

2. You are encountering new competitors that you didn't even dream of a few years earlier, and they are tough, price-slashing competitors that can rapidly deliver either a similar or the very same product or service to your customers.

3. You are taken for granted by the customers you have served for a period of time because they have been lulled into complacency through their total familiarity with your execution.

So what can you do?

Now that you understand what has created the collapse of distinction— from both organizational and individual standpoints—in the next chapter we will take a look at what creates differentiation in the marketplace, whether you are an executive at a global conglomerate, a professional seeking greater success, or an entrepreneur running a small-town diner.

Executive Summary

I. The Three Destroyers of Differentiation has an impact that is not limited to corporations.

    a. The destructive impact is also encountered by individual professionals trying to survive and thrive in their careers.

    b. No matter your occupation, you are threatened by the impact of the collapse of distinction.

II. Examination of Examples

    a. Financial services

        i. Just when you thought your ongoing tenure would mean a larger and growing book of business that you could easily maintain by matching the efforts of your competition; your clients now seem bored and distracted; they're seeking less costly online alternatives; it's harder to retain and obtain new clients; and in today's market, it's no fun on a personal basis anymore.

    b. Retail dry cleaners

        i. You've upgraded your stores and become environmentally conscious, yet, when your competition cuts their price, you do, too. You're working harder (for less money) and not enjoying it at all.

    c. What has created these problems?

        i. The Three Destroyers of Differentiation

III. The impact of the Three Destroyers on individual professionals

a. Destroyer #1: Copycat Competition

   i. You believed that by keeping pace with your competition, you would stay in the game.

   ii. Therefore, you emulated what they did—and they did the same to you.

   iii. The problem is that neither of you are now differentiated in any meaningful way from the other!

   iv. The Ric Flair example: "To be the man…"

      1. Most professionals take the least progressive, most conforming activity possible to achieve the minimum level of success personally acceptable

b. Destroyer #2: New Competition = New Challenges

   i. New competitors, arriving on your doorstep because of technological advances from the Interstate Highway to the Internet, are creating new challenges.

   ii. If you have failed at Destroyer #1, the dilemma presented here by Destroyer #2 is exacerbated.

      1. Not only are you non-differentiated from your existing competition, but now there are new players in the game offering faster or cheaper service!

2. And, if you've lived by the "price sword," you may now find that you are going to perish from it as well.

c. Destroyer #3: Customer Boredom

   i. Because "familiarity breeds complacency," if you approach customers in the same personal manner as you have been in the past, they are becoming bored with your approach and technique.

   ii. What have you changed in the past year in your approach to customers?

      1. If you can't think of an answer, then the response should be: "Nothing."

IV. The Trifecta!

   a. You are creating only incremental improvement, if any at all.

   b. You are encountering new competition you did not anticipate.

   c. You are taken for granted by your customers because you have lulled them into complacency.

V. You have discovered the intense personal impact of the Three Destroyers of Differentiation!

Action Steps, Questions, and Ideas

- Name specific steps in your career where the Destroyers of Differentiation have affected you.

- Do you want to "be the man" or woman? Are you willing to "beat the man" or woman to get there? Or are you content with achieving "good enough" status? Write a paragraph that explains your position, your intentions, and two action steps you will take.

- What have you changed in the past year to freshen your approach with your customers and colleagues?

Three

The Avenues of Differentiation

In the all-time classic film comedy from 1978, *National Lampoon's Animal House,* there is a statue at the legendary Faber College in Faber, Pennsylvania. Placed in front of the administration building, which houses the office of the evil Dean Vernon Wormer (played in the film to perfection by the late John Vernon), is a sculpture of the college's founder, the lead-pencil tycoon Emil Faber. Inscribed on the pedestal is the motto of this esteemed institution: "Knowledge is good."

Okay, I admit that I have a weird sense of humor, and that little witticisms make me laugh out loud. At Harvard, the motto is *Veritas*, "truth." At Yale, *Lux et veritas*, "light and truth." *Die Luft der Freiheit weht* is Stanford's unofficial motto and translates as "the wind of freedom blows." (The phrase is a quote from Ulrich von Hutten, a sixteenth-century humanist, as reported by the official Stanford Web site.)

My friend Dr. Nido Qubein is president of the rapidly growing High Point University in High Point, North Carolina. The institution over which he presides is directed by the phrase *Nil Sine Numine*, "nothing without divine guidance."

However, the illustrious (and fictional) Faber affirms the pseudo-profound statement that "knowledge is good."

In this chapter we'll examine a small portion of the theory behind three primary strategies for creating differentiation. These are concepts that I believe will provide significant light and truth—because, at the end of the day, "differentiation is good." Leaders of organizations are paid to select and direct the strategies that they believe will make their businesses more profitable. I hope you are beginning to see that no one can afford to overlook differentiation and still maintain any kind of competitive lead, regardless of the industry or size of their business.

But first, what is *differentiation*? And is it different from *distinction*? There is a lot of literature and discussion that uses these words, but what exactly do they mean? Since both terms are used here—and treated somewhat interchangeably—it might be easy to get confused.

There is an overlap in meaning, after all. Both terms mean that you have created clear advantages over your competition in the market. Both terms mean that you are executing strategies—individually and organizationally—that will either establish or maintain your ability to display to your customers and colleagues that they should prefer what you offer. Therefore, either term can mean the effort to set you and your organization apart from your competitors in a cluttered marketplace.

Where both terms differ is in their degree. They fall at different places along a continuum. Level one is *Sameness*, that "sea of similarity" my old-timer friend back home was discussing. This is the place where most organizations and the professionals who work for them are found adrift. They do not have characteristics that would compel their customers to be loyal and passionate about their products or services. They are the casualties of the destroyers of differentiation we discussed earlier.

Level two is *Differentiation*. Businesses and workers at this level are not satisfied with numbing similarity, and so display characteristics that set them apart from their competition. They will point to various aspects of their products and services and say, "See! This proves we are better than our rivals!" Beware, though: the unique points they are so proud of may not find traction with customers.

In my consulting business, I endlessly hear from organizations that direct me to their "friendly customer service" as being a point of differentiation—and, of course, their competitors claim exactly the same thing! If both you and your competition prove uniqueness by referring to identical characteristics, then *neither* of you is correct. There is no point of advantage. You are the same. And, just being "different" does not secure true "differentiation." If I slap every customer in the face, I may be truly different from my competition, but have I obtained the goodwill of my customers, prospects, and colleagues?

Finally, level three is *Distinction*. Because of the collapse we discussed in chapter one, this level is an extraordinarily rare place for individuals and organizations. Nevertheless, we all know professionals or companies who become the "go to" provider in any industry. They are so uncommonly excellent, or their differentiation strategies are executed to such an extraordinary level of precision, that these distinct examples become clear market leaders.

Consider the computer industry—and specifically the laptop market—and you can come up with a lot of names at level one (Sameness) with relative ease. Gateway, Acer, Hitachi, Fujitsu, Samsung, and so forth are the ones that first come to my mind. These manufacturers all seem to run together in a pack of similarity. I'm certain they make a fine product, and I know they usually charge a lower price. But it is difficult for me to find an exceptionally compelling reason to choose an Acer over a Gateway, as a case in point, because I'm just not aware of any points that assist in discriminating between them.

Level two (Differentiation) are those manufacturers that are known for something: HP laptops are media centers; Dell is built-to-order on a budget; Sony integrates their line of digital still and video cameras and other products into their Vaio units. Level two manufacturers all possess their unique points of differentiation, and so attempt to justify why you, the prospective customer, might choose to buy a Sony as opposed to a Dell, or vice versa. That's differentiation, and it generates the perception that purchasing an HP laptop, for example, is a superior choice and value than selecting a product from a company operating at level one, even though level one manufacturers sell at a lower price.

Level three (Distinction) is perhaps best represented today by Apple and its line of MacBooks. The Mac has become, to use the term of author and consultant Joe Calloway, a "category of one." The Mac has developed to the point that it no longer merely possesses points of differentiation, it has risen to a class it isn't just different from other personal computers, as created an emotional connection with its customers. Level three is where everyone, no matter what business or industry, wants to be. It is accomplished via a four-step process, which I will outline in a later chapter. You can do it, even if you or your organization is still languishing on level one. But you cannot do it without first attaining differentiation.

So then, any discussion of differentiation—and how that strategy enhances profitability—has to include one of the most important books ever written on the subject, Michael Porter's *Competitive Advantage: Creating and Sustaining Superior Performance.* Porter's is one of the first books that I examined as I began to study the subject, and I could not help noticing that most of the ongoing studies, researched by a vastly diverse field of academics, almost always mentioned his conclusions. Let's take a very brief look at a couple of Porter's concepts and see how we can build a framework to assist you in creating distinction for yourself and your organization.

Porter believes that businesses compete using three generic strategies.

1. *Cost leadership.* The ability to produce your goods and services less expensively than your competition, thereby providing you with an advantage.

2. *Focus.* The concentration of your resources and efforts upon a niche or segment in the marketplace where you believe you can sustain a competitive advantage.

3. *Differentiation.* Creating a point of uniqueness that, in
   turn, creates viable benefits diverse from the
   advantages of your competitors.

When it comes to differentiation, according to Porter, there
are really only three strategies that an organization can employ
to separate itself from the competition:

1. product differentiation

2. price differentiation, and

3. service differentiation.[1]

Let's briefly examine them and ask how you may execute these
strategies at your organization.

Product Differentiation

Product differentiation means that your organization is focused
on designing and manufacturing a product that is clearly unique
when compared to that of your competitors. This product must
be perceived to be so dissimilar that in and of itself it creates the
space your organization seeks in the market. This area of differentiation could be considered the "build-the-better-mousetrap"
strategy. The thinking here would be stated, "If our product is
significantly superior to our competition's, then we have developed a point of distinction in the marketplace."

Many better-quality products have achieved great distinction. The iPod attained superior market share because it was easier to use than other MP3 players already in circulation, it worked without hassle, and it had a coolness factor. Therefore, it is important to honestly ask yourself and your organization if the product you produce is exceptional enough to create differentiation between you and your competition. If not, then what are you going to *do* about it?

You have three choices: produce a differentiated product, pick another differentiation strategy, or do both!

Price Differentiation

Creating price differentiation is not necessarily promoting the cheapest price. It is *leveraging* the price you charge for your goods and services to the point that it becomes a strategic aspect of distinction.

Wal-Mart may be the first company that comes to mind when we consider price differentiation. With a corporate motto of "Save Money. Live Better," there's no doubt that Wal-Mart has determined that the price it charges for items ranging from Tide to automobile batteries has become a point where it can separate itself from the competition.

And the strategy has worked pretty darn well for the company, hasn't it? The approach would seem to lend credence to those researchers who advocate a solitary method as having the most impact in creating distinction.

However, automobile manufacturers such as Bentley and Rolls-Royce also have a price differentiation strategy. Charging a premium for their products establishes the perception of exclusivity, which, in turn, produces a special demand among the affluent prospects they target. And the value perception created, in part, by their price differentiation strategy creates a point of differentiation between Bentley and Rolls and other luxury manufacturers such as Mercedes and Lexus.

It's pretty obvious if you are a coffee drinker that Starbucks ain't the Wal-Mart of coffee. The price of their products is so well-known and discussed that it has become the fodder for everything from university research to comedians' monologues. However, the company's success appears to support those who are proponents of multiple strategies as being most effective in creating maximum differentiation. Despite their more recent challenges that we'll address later, Starbucks has certainly been a leader in price, service, and product selection in their industry.

Your price has to be a thoroughly designed tactic that creates differentiation to successfully employ this strategy. You can be cheaper, or you can be more expensive. However, it should be obvious that there is no differentiation in this area if your pricing is *similar* to that of your competitors. Is there is a coherent, congruent strategy in place regarding your price leveraged to the point that it becomes a factor of differentiation—or are you just playing the game of "me too" in the marketplace?

You have three choices: lower your price to the point that it separates you from the competition, raise your price to the point that it creates significant exclusivity, or select another method of differentiation.

Service Differentiation

How do you serve your customers and prospects? Is your service different from that of your competitors? Or is the industry standard to provide a modicum of convenience, based upon your perception of your customers' desires? How do they think of your service model, and is it in a style that provides you with a unique positioning in their minds?

Service differentiation does not necessarily imply we treat our customers *better* than our competition does. That is much too subjective. I have yet to discover the organization that doesn't offer at least lip service toward the subject of customer service. All professionals and companies will tell you that they deal with their customers in a service-oriented manner. (Even if too often their customers would love to tell them that they are wrong!)

Service differentiation means we deal with customers in a manner that is unique from our competition. And that difference produces points that set us apart to the extent that our customers continue to choose us over our competition.

In my hometown, parents had a choice of two places to take their sons to get a haircut. I always asked Mom to take me to Sweazy's Barber Shop because Dwight Sweazy always gave me a handful of candy after I got my hair cut. The other place was friendly, and the burr haircut (or crew cut) was pretty much the same at both shops. However, for a five-year-old boy, a fistful of suckers was the service differentiation required to create sustained customer loyalty.

What would it take to create service differentiation in your category? How could you execute a service strategy that would make customers and prospects perceive your entire efforts as differentiated? You have two options: (1) create a service strategy that customers find compelling enough to reward you with their business; or (2) hope that the product and/or the price will be distinctive enough that you can make up for your lack of service differentiation.

"Here in the Real World . . ."

One of my favorite recording artists is Alan Jackson. Jackson has won just about every award in the field, has sold tens of millions of CDs, and performs to sold-out arenas around the world before millions of adoring fans.

Alan Jackson's first hit was a terrific song titled, "Here in the Real World." The lyrics forlornly contrasted how romance is portrayed in the movies and on television with the everyday situations that normal people experience.

Just like Alan Jackson, you and I must deal with the real-life challenges of business here in the real world. We cannot change the product mix and profile of our organizations in most instances.

Even CEOs can have their hands tied when it comes to the product line. My guess is that even if you are selected as the next CEO of Apple to follow Steve Jobs, you aren't going to stop making Macs. If you are the CEO of a major hotel chain, you have no chance to turn it into anything else. You have too much invested in real estate and more to execute such a dramatic twist.

And many of us cannot impact the price strategy of our goods and services either. Sure, if you are booking professional speeches and lectures as I do, you could perhaps decide tomorrow to double your fee or to cut it in half. You may possibly have that freedom as an entrepreneur of a small enterprise—however, the vast majority of professionals lack that authority.

You already may have a firmly established position in the market based on your pricing. For example, do you remember when Wal-Mart made a short, ill-fated attempt to become a retailer of a few lines of premium-priced products? Their attempts to "out-Target" a competitor just didn't work. Wal-Mart is a company that is just too well recognized as the go-to place for "lower prices every day."

Frankly, I was a bit embarrassed for Mercedes sales professionals who had to retail that little low-end roller skate on wheels they called the A Class. The model was added to the Mercedes line in an attempt to sway buyers on the lower end of the price spectrum. I think the product diminished their brand and could have eroded their perception in the market.

Writing in *Automotive Magazine,* Mark Gillies stated in his review that the car was "a brilliant technical concept." However, he continued, "the desire to sell more cars sits, to me, uneasily, with the luster of the three-pointed star. In short, Mercedes has been devaluing one of the most respected hallmarks in the world in a Faustian swap for market share."[2] In other words, you can be one of the most respected manufacturers in your industry, but if you have been successful at creating differentiation using the price strategy, changing your policy can wound your brand.

If you are in financial services, you may have absolutely no control over pricing. Your product might be a mutual fund, for example, but the financial markets will always determine the price. You could fervently believe that your fund is undervalued, yet if the market doesn't agree, you have neither the ability nor the authority to arbitrarily change the pricing.

> **If you cannot impact the design of your products, and if you cannot choose or control the price, then your primary point of differentiation has to be in service.**

You shouldn't decry your lack of choice here, for (coincidentally or not) the strategy that can have the most significant impact on your organization and customers is the avenue most available to you. It is an approach that you can integrate into your planning and execute fairly rapidly, and it is a tactic that can create measurable long-term benefits for both customers and colleagues.

What Doesn't Work

Now that we have reviewed Michael Porter's differentiation strategies, let me suggest what will *not* differentiate you in today's world:

1. Product quality

2. Customer service

3. Differentiation strategy planning sessions

Product Quality

You might be saying, "Wait a minute! Scott, you just reported that product differentiation is one of the strategies that can develop competitive advantages. Now you are suggesting it does not?"

No, that's not what I'm saying. What I mean is that having a high-quality product—one that is manufactured with a minimum of defects, one that is built to last—is not a differentiating factor anymore. Granted, it *used* to be. There was a time years ago when building the highest-quality product would make customers stand up and take notice, and prospects would sprint to your side. No longer.

The reason is that your competitors have improved their product, just as you have. Companies have well-manufactured products to sell now; otherwise, they would be out of business. And given the rapid, vapor-like life cycle of products in many industries today, it does not take long for a competitor who may be behind to catch up with you.

"Think about Hewlett-Packard LaserJet printers. Time was, they owned the office and high-end home computer printer markets. They were fast, clean, and made documents look slick. HP printers were the best, and the company was so fast to market that its sole competition was its own next wave of printers," writes Ron Jonash, vice president and director of technology and innovation management consulting practice at Arthur D. Little, a management consulting firm based in Cambridge, Massachusetts. "Then Epson, Canon, and Lexmark caught up and joined the party, and suddenly competition in PC printers wasn't based on winning features, innovation, or service [anymore]."

He continues:

Competitors copy success. Reverse engineering a laser printer or hard drive and then gearing up production takes less time than ever. What starts out as original thinking doesn't last long. Patents and copyrights and intellectual property protection only go so far. . . . New product lifecycles for telecommunications devices and personal computer printers are measured in months.[3]

A better burger was not the answer to Alvie Kern's problem at his small-town diner. Product quality was not the issue; he had great food. It just wasn't enough for him to enable his small business to survive.

Don't get me wrong. You must have product quality. You are *doomed* without it. Just don't believe for a moment that it will differentiate you or your organization.

Customer Service

"Okay," you're thinking, "I've got you on this one! You are clearly making the point that the vast majority of us cannot control the product or the price, so service is the only thing that is left. How can you claim customer service will fail to differentiate?"

To a degree, I plead "guilty as charged." Service is all that is left. I make this point to drive home the assertion that ordinary, run-of-the-mill customer service does nothing to make you distinct.

Consider the tourist industry in the beautiful country of New Zealand. They embarked upon a "Kiwi-friendly" effort to improve the level of customer service for visitors and then evaluated those travelers' responses to the service of which they were the supposed beneficiaries. The results showed that "only one in three people are satisfied" with the customer service.

A survey of nearly 400 people by service training organization KiwiHost found that 67 per cent of people did not get the service they wanted. . . . KiwiHost managing director Simon Nikoloff said the key finding was that service providers *simply did not understand what a customer wanted*. A smile and a hello simply did not do the trick. A willingness to help, listening and understanding, and taking responsibility to help were the three outstanding gripes consumer and business customers detailed.

"We think being Kiwi-friendly is enough; the reality is that people are looking for some grunt behind that," Nikoloff said.[4]

Customer service—as traditionally defined—didn't keep the doors of Kern's Grill open, either. Alvie's daughter and wife were friendly, and you didn't have to wait long to receive your order.

If you define customer service as being friendly, answering the phone quickly, moving the customer through the transaction process efficiently, and all of the other nonsense to which managers have subscribed for way too long, then you may be a nice person or organization, but you are miles away from creating the type of customer *experience* that will differentiate your organization. In a later chapter I'll outline what you need to do to create a customer experience that differentiates.

Differentiation Strategy Planning Sessions

And that little word—*do*—leads us to the next point that will fail to create differentiation. I have attended, and on several occasions facilitated, countless numbers of strategic planning sessions designed to examine the topic of differentiation, look at methods by which an organization can create it, and engineer processes by which it can be executed within the company.

Guess what? Most of the time these sessions don't result in any positive change!

The reason is simple: *planning* differentiation is not *doing* differentiation!

EUCG, Inc. (formerly known as the Electric Utility Cost Group) reported that author and business consultant Sam Geist told attendees at the fall conference in October 2007 exactly that when he said, "Execution of a corporate strategy is more funda-mental to the success of a company than the strategy itself. Without executing the strategy, nothing happens—ideas and plans disintegrate. Organizations have the propensity to strategize first, then worry about execution as a mere afterthought." Geist also noted, "This is often a setup for failure. Companies should first formulate an objective, vision, or goal and then develop the execution plan to achieve it. Execution is the strategy."[5]

I'm fairly certain the entire Kern family talked about what they should do to face the challenges confronting their little diner. I remember Alvie even asking my dad what he thought they should do. Alvie Kern pondered long and hard about what steps he should take, he discussed the issue with his family, and he sought advice from other small business owners in our rural community. Then he went back to doing what he had always done.

I love the line from Sam Geist: *execution is the strategy*. Examining the behavior of many organizations, you could infer that the strategy is to meet, not to act. Again, the reason is simple: it is easier—and perceived to be less risky—to *meet* about differentiation than it is to *execute* differentiation.

> Make a difference for yourself
> and your organization by creating
> a difference!

Step Up!

During this time of the collapse of distinction, you must step up and create points of uniqueness for your organization and yourself. Because, just like Faber College's motto about knowledge, we know now that differentiation is *"good."*

In the next chapter, we'll take a look at the fundamental principle that unlocks the secret—explaining why this phenomenon has such traction in the marketplace and providing insight for your efforts.

Executive Summary

I. The three levels of business or professional differentiation are:

a. Level One: Sameness

i. This is the point where you or your organization is fundamentally indistinguishable from your competition from the customer's point of view.

    ii. Companies or professionals at this level do not have characteristics compelling enough to generate loyalty or passion regarding their products or services.

       1. Chapter examples in the computer industry are Acer, Gateway, Hitachi, and Fujitsu

  b. Level Two: Differentiation

    i. You or your business display traits that set you apart from your competitor.

    ii. This distinguishing aspects may—or may not—gain traction for you in the marketplace.

    iii. If you and your competition claim similar aspects as your point of differentiation, such as "customer service," the result is that there is little or no true differentiation from the customer's perspective.

       1. Examples from the chapter in computers are Sony, Dell, and HP.

  c. Level Three: Distinction

    i. You are the primary provider in your field. You are on the mind of you customer in a significant and meaningful manner.

    ii. So uncommonly excellent that you have a clear leadership position.

      iii. Organizations and individuals operating at this level are what author Joe Calloway categorizes as a "category of one."

        1. The example from the chapter is Apple.

II. According to Michael Porter's "Competitive Advantage," there are three generic strategies to creating differentiation:

  a. Product

    i. The "build a better mousetrap" strategy

    ii. Your product is significantly superior in the marketplace

  b. Price

    i. The strategy where the price of your products or services creates space in the marketplace between you and your competition.

    ii. Most initially consider this to mean low price, such as how Wal-Mart created differentiation from its competitors.

    iii. However, the price differentiation strategy can also mean a higher price, such as how Rolls Royce creates space in the market from Mercedes-Benz.

  c. Service

    i. Service differentiation doesn't necessarily mean we treat our customers better—it should mean that we treat them *uniquely*.

       1. "Better" is too subjective—and will be claimed as a differentiating factor by almost all.

III. In the real world, Service is the primary differentiating choice.

    a. Most of us cannot determine the price of our product or service.

    b. Nor can we completely decide what we are building and selling.

    c. However, organizationally—and individually—we can have an immediate and profound impact upon how our customers are treated.

    d. If you cannot impact the design of your products, and cannot choose or control the price, then your primary point of differentiation *must* be found in service.

IV. What will always fail to differentiate you and your organization?

    a. Product quality

       i. If your product isn't one of quality, you are probably already out of business in today's hyper-competitive market.

    b. Customer service

       i. *Yes!* Service makes a compelling difference.

       ii. However, ordinary, run-of-the-mill, "be friendly and smile" customer service is so bland and undistinguished that it will create little to no traction for you or your organization.

   c. Differentiation strategy planning sessions

      i. The key is to move beyond planning into execution.

      ii. Planning sessions do not generate differentiation.

         1. Moving from the sessions into actual practice is where true differentiation is created.

V. Now is the time for organizations (and profound professionals) to step up and create points of uniqueness.

Action Steps, Questions, and Ideas

- My barber used suckers as a service strategy for young boys to continue to get haircuts from him. What strategy keeps your customers returning for more?

- What is your differentiation strategy? List ten things that would be proof of the execution of the strategy.

Four

The Ebert Effect

Why did Ted's Restaurant survive—and even thrive—when Kern's Grill did not? What was it about these two small-town Indiana diners that caused one to fold under the pressure, to yield to the Three Destroyers of Differentiation? What made the difference?

After all, both restaurants were so much alike. Kern's had fried onions on its double-decker burger, while Ted's had Thousand Island dressing, sure, but their prices were about the same. The fried chicken platter with mashed potatoes and gravy cost equally as much at either place.

Was it the service? Well, maybe. Both places waited on you in a timely and efficient manner. Both places put the food on the table fairly quickly. Nevertheless, for some reason Ted's was a place where you wanted to linger while Kern's was the diner where you most likely chose to eat and run. In other words, while *service* was efficient in both places, the *experience* was significantly different at Ted's. Certainly, McDonald's, Wendy's, Burger King, and all of the other entrants into the fast-food arena created speedy service and undoubtedly with their resources became superior at its execution over Kern's and Ted's. Yet it was *just different* at Ted's.

The purpose of this chapter is to reveal a powerful principle that illuminates why it is so important for any organization or professional to create differentiation. And, unlike most significant business tenets, this one was discovered through an interaction with a famous movie critic! This concept will explain why one business can survive while another in the same industry will succumb—why one professional attains a high level of respect and recognition, while another with similar qualifications remains mired in a stagnant career.

Why is "just different" so important? Because in today's marketplace, different is better! (At least customers certainly perceive it that way.)

The Ebert Effect

In one of my earlier books, *ALL Business Is Show Business*, I described the fortunate set of circumstances that enabled me to play the role of the villain in the highly regarded German movie

Stroszek and my work with the esteemed director Werner Herzog. (I play the young Wisconsin banker who repossesses the German immigrant family's mobile home.) This marvelous event in my life later afforded me another unlikely opportunity—to become a film critic, with my commentaries syndicated to eighty television stations across the U.S. and around the world.

Several years ago, I attended a reception in Hollywood for movie reviewers that was sponsored by one of the major studios. There I had the occasion to meet the best in the business, Roger Ebert. You are probably aware of his incredible body of work—from his reviews that started in the *Chicago Sun-Times* in 1967, to the Emmy-nominated *Siskel & Ebert & the Movies* that continued until Gene Siskel's passing in 1999, to *At the Movies with Ebert & Roeper*. To my delight and surprise, the famed critic remembered the terrific review he gave my solitary attempt at acting. In fact, he featured *Stroszek* as one of his "Great Films" series of articles, and he has often noted that it is one of the "best films ever made you have never heard of." Roger asked me to sit with him and his wife, and we began a warm and fascinating conversation.

He asked me what had most surprised me about reviewing films. My response was that I could not understand why so many critics offered such glowing reviews to so many foreign films that seemed, to me, to be amateurish in their script and production. I jokingly told him I thought "many of the critics in the room would have loved *Texas Chainsaw Massacre*—if it had only been produced with subtitles!"

Roger chuckled, then shocked me a bit with his response, which first came in the form of a question: "Scott, how many movies are you normally seeing in any given week?" "One," I answered, meaning the solitary film I would be reviewing for that week's broadcast.

"Don't you see? That's your problem," he responded. "Many of the people in this profession are seeing one or two movies a *day*! Those little, offbeat, quirky, odd foreign or independent films—like the one you are in, *Stroszek*—they capture our attention because they are a bit different! When you are overwhelmed with such boring similarity, you begin to perceive that *different is better!*"

That remarkable, Pulitzer Prize–winning journalist and critic taught me a great business lesson I now call the Ebert Effect:

The Ebert Effect: When people, from their perspective, are inundated with indistinguishable choices, they perceive a product, service, approach, or experience with a specific point of differentiation to be superior.

By the way, I continue to learn from Roger Ebert. My wife, Tammy, and I were invited to be his guests at his film festival, Ebertfest, at the University of Illinois in the summer of 2007. Roger selected *Stroszek* to be one of the main features of his event—and I was reunited with director Herzog after thirty years. More important, we witnessed Roger's valiant battle with cancer and his extraordinary courage and commitment. He is an amazing individual with remarkable insight well beyond his considerable expertise in film.

Expand the Ebert Effect from entertainment and film to your business. How many insurance companies are there, for example? And how many differing types of policies are each of these companies offering? The number is overwhelming, both to the industry and, more importantly, to customers.

How many mid-sized, mid-priced sedans sit in automobile showrooms? Could you begin to count the number of non-differentiated dealerships employing a mass of indistinguishable salespeople executing a generic sales process to sell those cars?

Consider all of the companies attempting to market everything from copiers to computers, from equipment to engineering, to your organization. Have you ever pondered the sheer number of groups out there trying to sell something to your business? Do you ever wonder why, from this myriad of marketers, you choose only a few, select vendors? (And, do you wonder how *you* can become that "provider of choice" to the groups that you are targeting?)

On how many occasions have you blandly been treated like a number, or interchangeable part, whether the transaction was as a retail consumer or part of a business-to-business sale?

It is a given that in today's world there are an overwhelming number of options available to customers. If all of those choices appear similar, then displaying attributes that are original will mean—according to the Ebert Effect—that clients and prospects will begin to perceive you not only as different, but *superior*, as well.

What the Ebert Effect Means to You

The Ebert Effect has many points of impact for you and your organization. Here are some of the most significant:

- It doesn't matter that you believe your product, service, or self is distinctive. The *only* perception that matters is the customers'.

- Although the product you sell may be incrementally enhanced over that of your competition, if you are perceived to be just another brick in a wall of sameness, your modest superiority gains you little to no traction with customers.

- If you serve your customers in a similar manner to that of your competition, you dramatically erode your product's advantages, because you have contributed to becoming indistinguishable.

- You may be so busy doing your job for your organization, you overlook—or even ignore—the sheer volume of similar messages that your customers are receiving.

• Creating differentiation doesn't mean you have to become completely, totally unique from your competition from top to bottom. It simply means *you must create small, solid points of distinction* that are recognizable and important from the customers' perspective because customers perceive that different is better.

Why Ted's Survived

Once we understand the Ebert Effect, it becomes easier to hypothesize why Ted's remained a viable business, while Kern's Grill went under. Both were serving the same market—a small, rural town in southern Indiana. Both were serving basically the same menus. It was not a situation where one was serving Chinese food and the other was offering Italian cuisine, making it possible to suggest that the results were influenced by the culinary choices of the owner. Both had engaged proprietors and families, providing good food with good service at a reasonable price.

However, while Kern's Grill attempted, as mentioned earlier, to "out-McDonald's McDonald's," Ted's continued to be the place where customers wanted to hang around. And because there was a divergence in the experience, customers perceived a superior differentiation and responded accordingly. Customers regarded Ted's as unique and different from the drive-through fast-food establishments. They considered that Kern's was trying to keep pace with a train that had already left the station.

In other words, that little difference *was* the difference, even to the point of the life and death of the business itself.

The Four Cornerstones of Distinction

Through my research and experience, I've discovered that there are Four Cornerstones of Distinction. Every company and person must draw upon these qualities to develop differentiation and uniqueness in the marketplace. These cornerstones will, at first, appear to be elemental. However, the more you study them—and what it requires to be successful at each—the more you will realize how spectacularly challenging it is to execute them.

When you think about it, though, this paradox may also answer an important question: Why is it so rare to see *true* differentiation? The answer is that we

1. do not recognize or understand these cornerstones,
2. fail to develop and implement the strategies necessary to execute the cornerstones,
3. or *both*.

The great news, however, is that any organization or professional can change this situation *instantly*. As you discover the Cornerstones of Distinction, you can immediately begin to plan how you will harness their power.

The Four Cornerstones of Distinction are:

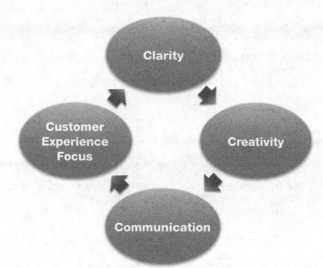

The following chapters will explore each of these cornerstones and explain how you can develop strategies that will create distinction in the marketplace.

Executive Summary

 I. Why one and not the other?

  a. In the example of my hometown diners, one died a quick death in the face of new competition, but the other survived.

  b. Why does one business succeed when the other fails?

c. What is the difference between survival and extinction?

II. The Ebert Effect

a. Famed film critic Roger Ebert once told me that while I was seeing one movie a week, he often saw two a day—every day!

i. He noted that often meant that movies that were different or unique in some manner would catch his attention and generate a positive response.

b. The Ebert Effect is: "When people, from their perspective, are inundated with indistinguishable choices, they perceive a product, service, approach, or experience with a specific point of differentiation to be superior."

III. What this means to you

a. The Ebert Effect has many points of impact, however, perhaps the most important are:

i. Creating differentiation does not mean you have to change everything and become completely unique from your competition.

ii. It means you must create *small, solid points* that are recognizable as different and important from the customer's perspective.

      iii. From today's customer's point of view, different IS superior.

IV. The Four Cornerstones of Distinction

    a. There are four basic points that create the foundation of distinction.

    b. These points appear simple, however, most organizations either fail to execute them, or fail to recognize them.

      i. The usual result is being trapped at Level One (Sameness) with no plan of advancement.

    c. These Four Cornerstones must be implemented—in their specific order—to create distinction for your organization and yourself.

    d. The Four Cornerstones of Distinction are:

      i. Clarity

      ii. Creativity

      iii. Communication

      iv. Customer Experience Focus

Action Steps, Questions, and Ideas

- Keeping in mind the Ebert Effect, list five points where customers would regard you and/or your organization as being different from everything else they see in the marketplace.

- Why do you believe it is so rare to see true differentiation?

- What can you do about it for yourself and your organization?

Five

The First Cornerstone: Clarity

There are four basic qualities that every business and each professional must draw upon to develop exceptional merit in the marketplace. These are the Four Cornerstones of Distinction. The next four chapters will examine each cornerstone, and prescribe some approaches so you can build distinction for yourself and your organization.

The Four Cornerstones of Distinction are:

- Distinction is created by developing Clarity
- Distinction is created by developing Creativity

- Distinction is created by developing Communication
- Distinction is created by developing a Customer-Experience Focus

Cornerstone One: Clarity

A song that may often play in your living room was the title track of a 1978 album by the legendary rock band the Who. It's from the group's final record with drummer Keith Moon before his untimely passing from a drug overdose. This rock classic was written by the Who's guitarist, Pete Townsend, and undoubtedly, he is still cashing big royalty checks from its success. Now the theme music for one of the top-rated television shows in America, *CSI: Crime Scene Investigation* on CBS, this venerable work is, of course, "Who Are You?"

To some degree this tune is playing in customers' heads when they deal with you and your organization. *What I really want to know,* they chant in their method and manner, *is who are you?*

Why Is That So Hard to Answer?

I'm constantly asking entrepreneurial professionals and organizational managers that question: "Who are you? How would you specifically define yourself and your company?" And guess what? Most cannot answer that question.

By asking, "Who are you?" I do not mean your title, the company's name, or the name of the product you manufacture or sell. The answer I'm seeking goes much, much deeper. I w[...] know what is compelling about you, what will create points of distinction about you, and what will establish a connection between us?

Here is the reason that many—and I suggest *most*—organizations and professionals cannot answer the question: they do not have *clarity* about who they really are.

> **Many organizations and professionals are so afraid of losing to the competition, they strive to become almost all things to almost all people, believing it will bring them more customers.**

Play a game sometime with someone in financial services, for example. All you have to do is to innocently ask, "What do you do?" Chances are, he will respond with a litany of products—"I insure your future with a variety of mutual funds, annuities, IRAs, and other investment instruments, as well as provide total financial solutions including everything from mortgages to retirement planning"—or he will respond with the hot catchphrase for the current market: "I'm a wealth manager." (Some may say "wealth advisor.")

Here's the problem. In the first instance, he isn't telling you *who he is;* he is informing you *what he sells.* And in the second instance, he is really saying the same thing! All you have to do with someone in the second group is to follow up with, "How much wealth does one have to invest to become the recipient of your management and advice?" He will probably view this as an opening and respond, "With a minimum of $100,000 [or $250,000 or $500,000, or whatever number he feels comfortable throwing out] I assist my clients by providing [ready for this?] a variety of mutual funds, annuities, IRAs, and other investment instruments, as well as providing total financial solutions including everything from mortgages to retirement planning." They're the *same;* it's just that the second version is slightly more sophisticated—or maybe it's merely slick.

Although this example focuses on one industry, I don't believe the situation is remarkably different in any other field. Abundant auto dealers want to accentuate the accoutrements of the car, believing that constitutes their business, rather than develop a driver's delight. Countless chefs center on their culinary creations instead of the real purpose of business—developing and enhancing customer connections. And plentiful pharmacists pontificate on pills—because their training has centered on them—rather than become passionate about patients. Let me be abundantly emphatic:

Who you are is *not* what you sell!

Has Clarity Become Counterintuitive?

The problem for many is that this point about clarity seems counterintuitive. "Come on," the standard response goes, "look at all the cliché companies—the ones you business authors always seem to cite. Southwest is really air travel, getting people from one point to another. Apple is really just computers and MP3 players. Starbucks is really nothing more than a glorified coffee shop."

After hearing this argument over an extended period of time, I have realized that this diatribe always derives from non-distinct organizations, or from individuals representing a non-distinct company. They always want to blame someone or something else, and they make comments like these:

> "If R & D just gave us the next iPod, everything would be fine."

> "If our frontline people were as good with customers as Southwest's, we would be doing great too."

> "If our management gave us insurance and stock options like Starbucks, we would work harder for the customers."

R & D *can't* give you the next iPod because it *doesn't know* what the company or its customers really want! This occurs because neither your customers nor anyone in your organization knows what the heck the company is all about. Henry Ford was reported to have said that you cannot depend *solely* upon customers to tell you what they really want. As he related, "If I would have asked people what they wanted, they would have answered, 'Faster horses.'" Ford, however, had clarity about what he wanted his company to become and, therefore, about what he wanted to build and market.

You can take the same flight attendants who made Southwest unique and put them to work for your organization, and they will flounder because there isn't clarity regarding what unites their efforts.

You can have insurance and options out the wazoo, but if you aren't clear with your people about what really matters, you won't end up with Starbucks. Instead, you'll have well-insured, well-optioned wandering generalities for employees.

Not as Easy as You Might Imagine

It's just flat-out difficult to discipline our organizations and ourselves to first discover, and then be clear about who and what we are. My experience is that it is incredibly more challenging than most companies and professionals anticipate. Part of why this is so tough is that being clear about who you are also commands that you possess clarity about who you are *not*!

> Clarity means that you are precise about who you are—and just as exact about who you are not!

It is easy to stand by generalities and modify them so that you don't lose the attention of prospective customers. In my experience, for example, many financial advisors have stated that their practice focuses on a precise target so they may understand the specific needs of that group. This, naturally, would enable the advisors to provide a special and distinct service. Then, however, people who fail to fit the target profile come along and want to invest—and the advisors take their business anyway!

When I ask them why they moved away from the clarity that would provide distinction, these sophisticated professionals say in all seriousness, "But what if they win the lottery and I had turned them away?" Good grief! If that is now the standard, these advisors should start prospecting at convenience stores because that is where most winning tickets are sold.

People always respond to this by asking me if this "clarity stuff" means that an organization or professional should turn away customers.

The answer is *yes*!

As you discover the other Cornerstones of Distinction, you will come to understand that truly differentiated organizations *never* try to attract everyone, and through their clarity, they take themselves out of the running for the business of some potential customers.

Take a look at what Starbucks is doing right now. It is common knowledge that the Starbucks brand is having trouble. So much so that its CEO, Howard Schultz, announced that "over the years we kind of lost our way." His company had attempted to become too many things to too many people. Serving breakfast sandwiches, for example, isn't really what Starbucks is supposed to be about. People wanting a hot breakfast sandwich should not have become a target customer for Starbucks. Once the company lost focus, you had to wonder: Where will it end? What's next—burgers for lunch? No! If you want a burger, go to Wendy's. And if a gourmet coffee drink like a latte or cappuccino is what you seek at midday, then Wendy's *should fire you* from its target lunch prospects.

To regain its distinctiveness in the market, Starbucks has made some interesting decisions. On the very day that I am writing this, Starbucks has closed nearly every store in the entire chain—7,100 locations—for three hours to give managers the opportunity to tell their baristas—their employees—who Starbucks *really* is. As Janet Adamy reported in the Wall Street Journal on February 27, 2008,

> At a Starbucks in downtown Chicago, about a dozen workers slurped samples of coffee and discussed how it smelled. They explained to each other how they conversed with their regular customers while managers gave them pointers on how to improve the interaction. Some of the Chicago baristas told managers they sometimes feel too rushed to give customers the best service and that they have difficulty remembering regular customers' names. "It should be a wow factor," said Andrew Alfano, regional vice president for Starbucks Midwest region.[1]

Would you have the guts to shut down your business— *system-wide*—for three hours to make certain there is clarity throughout your organization about who you really are, and what that means to customers?

The Example of Obama

Major national campaigns that candidates undertake for political office are, in fact, big businesses seeking to convert prospects (called citizens) into customers/voters. Perhaps no political operation in the history of our nation overcame greater odds, or was executed as flawlessly, as the presidential campaign of our nation's new leader, Barack Obama.

It's important to note that an appreciation of the manner in which President Obama organized and executed his campaign is not intended to be an endorsement (or rejection) of his policies. Any professional or company should possess an open mind toward learning from one of the best-managed organizations in recent memory, regardless of your political persuasion.

When Obama announced his campaign from the steps of the Illinois Old State Capitol—the same spot where Abraham Lincoln gave his "house divided" speech in 1858—he was perceived to be just one of the many challengers to the presumptive nominee of the Democratic party, former First Lady Hillary Rodham Clinton.

However, Obama understood how the "Ebert Effect" would work to his benefit. Just by being different from the candidates who had been around before—Clinton, John Edwards, Joe Biden, and Chris Dodd—there was a percentage of the electorate that would perceive him as a superior choice from the beginning.

Most important, though, is that any examination of the precise manner in which Barack Obama's candidacy was differentiated from those of his competitors, first in the Democratic primaries, then in the general election versus John McCain, displays a comprehensive implementation of the Four Cornerstones.

Barack Obama understood and implemented the first Cornerstone: Clarity. As David Brody, Senior National Correspondent for CBN (Christian Broadcasting Network) News, reported the night of the historic election, "There are several reasons why Barack Obama won the 2008 presidential election. But let me tell you in one simple sentence why he triumphed: Barack Obama will become the next President of the United States because he defined himself early with a *clear* message." (emphasis added)[2]

While other candidates were running all over Iowa and New Hampshire offering their viewpoints on Iraq, the economy, the Bush administration, and assorted other topics, Barack Obama's message was simple, profound and clear: He was the candidate of hope and change. When he expressed his positions on the issues other candidates were tackling, Obama almost always presented his points as seen through the prism of "hope and change."

Looking back, it's hard to remember a short, powerful phrase that describes any other candidate's efforts. Obama's clearness emphasized the power of his message—and accelerated his rise to the top. When the Democratic primaries were narrowed down to two major candidates from the eight that began the process, Hillary Clinton's higher name recognition was muted by the clarity of Barack Obama's message.

By the time John McCain had secured his party's nomination, it was too late for him to position himself as the leader for change that would have enabled him to distance himself from the unpopular Bush administration. Barack Obama clearly owned the "change" message, and it was one that voters plainly desired to hear.

"Well, We Are That *Too*"

While I'm writing this book, I'm also doing a series of consulting assignments with multimillion-dollar producers who are affiliated with the largest financial service brokerage in the country. As a result of the research developed with my good friend Dr. Rick Jensen of the Performance Center, located at PGA National Resort in Parkland, Florida, we know that the highest performing financial advisors have developed highly specialized practices and extraordinary clarity regarding their points of distinction in the marketplace. In eight separate meetings in a single day, I asked, "What differentiates your practice from those of other financial advisors?" Six times I received the response, "We provide great client service." Twice, the answer was, "I don't know."

Consider that for a moment; these are *successful* professionals! Granted, they aren't the best of the best, but they aren't failures, either. Yet somehow they have missed the point that if they want to achieve higher levels of success and profitability, the most important step they can take is to make their practice differentiated from the scores of others in the same business. Do they really think that "great client service" is a differentiator? Does that mean that others in their industry are indicating that they provide "pretty awful client service" to their investors? I doubt it.

I then asked them to describe their best client or most likely prospect. Some said, "Surgeons." Others responded with, "corporate executives" or professionals in other positions of affluence. However, when I asked the advisors who stated the targets and specialty of their practice to be "surgeons" if they would also accept as a client a corporate CEO who wanted to invest $250,000, *all* of them responded, "Well, we are that *too!*"

The problem is, you cannot be "that *too!*" and become distinct in your field. The top financial advisors I have worked with are highly specialized. They work only with surgeons. Rick Jensen knows one who works only with PGA golfers and another who works only with people involved in the sport of polo. If you have a pool of cash to invest, but are not a part of the polo scene, this advisor will refer you to someone else. (And, according to Dr. Jensen, he *has!*) By the way, Rick Jensen also reports that by turning away the business that is not a good fit, they have become among the most profitable of all professionals in their industry.

If I focus on surgeons, for example, as my clearly defined client base, I can learn their schedules, participate in their charitable activities, understand their unique professional challenges, educate myself in some of their specialized terminology, host client events that appeal to their specific needs, plan my work hours to fit the times that are easiest to contact them—and be contacted by them—and much more. However, this also answers why so few in any (and every) profession are able to attain significant distinction. Can you begin to imagine how difficult it is to learn all of this and more about a specific customer base? Therefore, we end up—organizationally and individually—knowing our products, but not our customers. We're often a mile wide and an inch deep when it comes to knowing what would really make a difference for the very people we seek to serve. Or we try to serve so many that we end up truly engaging very few.

The truth is you don't have enough time or energy to create highly distinctive customer experiences for a widely varied assembly of wildly diverse customers.

On the other hand, you might say that Wal-Mart sells "everything to everybody"—but that would not be accurate. What if you want a tuxedo? What about a designer gown? You cannot find them at Wal-Mart. Marketing low prices every day on mass-market consumer items is clearly what Wal-Mart is all about. There is a sizable amount of clarity regarding who the company is, even though it handles thousands of items.

Part of the reason that clarity is so vital is that you cannot distinguish a generic. Professionals simply cannot provide the kind of clarity and intense differentiation required for ultimate success if their focus is diluted. In the field of medicine, for example, we take for granted that the specialist is more highly compensated than the general practitioner. Usually, specialists are not the ones giving referrals to the GPs; it's the other way around. Why would we presume that other industries would have a different set of rules?

How Do You Become Clear?

If you are not clear, you have to get there. One of the best exercises I've developed for clarity stems from an approach that I related in my first business book, *ALL Business Is Show Business*. It's called the high concept principle. This isn't original to me. High concept is a principle that Hollywood and the entertainment industry have long understood as vital for creating and marketing their products.

For example, the concept—or plot—of a movie would tell you what that movie is all about. However, Hollywood recognized that people today have neither the time nor the inclination to listen to a long, involved concept or plot. The high concept is a short, powerful phrase that grabs and involves your audience. I can say, "Bomb on a bus," and you think of the movie *Speed*. "Shark attack!" elicits the response of *Jaws*. For the entertainment industry that potential audience is you and me. For your business the audience is your customers and prospects.

One new development has occurred since I first wrote about this approach years ago. Now Hollywood occasionally makes the title of the movie the *same* as the high concept. Not long ago, there was a Samuel L. Jackson movie called *Snakes on a Plane*. You don't have to wonder what that movie is about. If you were sitting in the theater and were astonished to see *snakes* on the *plane*, you were not paying attention as you walked past the ticket seller and the movie posters. There is a huge degree of clarity regarding that movie.

Visionary companies in today's entertainment-oriented times understand that this very principle works not just for movies but for their organizations. Here's an example: "Your pizza in thirty minutes!"

What company did you think of? Of course, Domino's!

I don't believe that anyone has ever picked up the phone to call Domino's because it is the all-time, best-tasting pizza that the customer has ever consumed. I believe that customers call Domino's because the company provides a darn good pizza that is delivered rapidly. That's a factor of distinction! And it is marketable, repeatable, recognizable, and referable for a simple reason: it is clear. Domino's knows who it is.

Domino's makes really, really good pizza, but it is not attempting to be a gourmet pizza establishment like Wolfgang Puck's Spago in Beverly Hills. Instead, the people at Domino's are clear that their factor of distinction is that they deliver a really good pizza to you very rapidly.

The Personal High Concept

Following my presentation to a group of successful financial consultants, one of the attendees asked me to review the high concept statement he had prepared. It was this: "I will help secure your financial future."

My response to his effort was to smile and say, "Boring!" His high concept failed to be interesting because every financial consultant from the newest life insurance salesperson to a very senior wealth manager with the esteemed Goldman Sachs could make an identical statement. His high concept had no degree of uniqueness. As we discussed the importance of distinction, he related to me that he was, in fact, now beginning his second career. In his first he was an air force fighter pilot. I told him to use that unique personal and professional aspect in his high concept statement; it would make him distinct.

His individual high concept is now this: "I fly clients through today's *financial* turbulence!" My response to that? "Exciting!" Wouldn't you want to know more?

Creating Your High Concept

Consider some fundamental questions as you develop your high concept statement:

- What makes your business (or you) *different* from your competition?
- What makes you *better* than your competition?
- What makes you and your organization *unique*?

If you cannot answer these questions, neither can your customers or employees.

Many "old style" sales training programs discussed a point they titled the "unique selling proposition" (USP). Every salesperson in the course was instructed to clearly classify what made their sales proposal inimitable to the customer. Back in those days, however, this USP usually centered on a specific feature or fact about the product. In today's world, the product approach has a diminished degree of value because customers focus less on the facts about the products and more on their customer experience and on how they feel about dealing with you. Your high concept should be a concise statement, but it does not need to be limited to a specific product or service.

Continue to develop your high concept by asking your colleagues and yourself these questions: What are the defining values of our organization? Are they outlined in our mission statement? Could they form the basis of our high concept statement?

Next, brainstorm a high concept with your colleagues. Then ask this question: are these the same points our customers would make about us? If they are, you are on your way!

Finally, here's a role-playing exercise. Ask your colleagues after your brainstorming session: how are the responses we've given different from those that our competition would provide? If they're not different, neither your high concept nor your organization is truly unique!

Not Just for the Entire Organization

The idea of a high concept is not limited to a broad application throughout the total organization.

As I've suggested, individuals need a high concept as a starting point on the road to the clarity necessary to build distinction. In addition, if you are seeking to create distinction for your department, for example, within your company, the high concept is a terrific place to begin.

Several years ago, I was the keynote speaker for the annual meeting of the American Payroll Association, which is led by their dynamic and highly creative CEO, Dan Maddux. The challenge I addressed for the group was that most employees in their departments would probably define their jobs as merely "cutting payroll checks." Let's face it; few people become motivated and excited about going to the office and creating distinction by simply "cutting checks." Now, several of the payroll departments of the organizations in attendance have signs on the walls of their offices with their new, distinctive high concept: "We deposit the money that funds the dreams of thousands of families—including our own!" They're not merely cutting checks; they're *funding dreams!*

There's no doubt that many will read about the high concept and consider the output of the exercise to be futile in today's volatile economy. They'll state that this is corny and childish—platitudes for the employees that accomplish little in the way of profitability and sales. I obviously disagree. I believe this to be the *starting point of distinction.*

You cannot differentiate what you cannot define!

Back in the days when it was called Federal Express, the company's employees clearly understood what the company was all about: getting a package from one customer to another absolutely, positively overnight. If an employee saw a misplaced package sitting on the dock, would he whimsically state, "Oh, well! We'll get it there tomorrow! Better late than never!"? Of course not! He would move heaven and earth to get the package where it was supposed to go—at the time it was supposed to be there—because it was abundantly clear who the organization was! The company delivered absolutely, positively overnight.

Has the FedEx of today altered itself a bit? Certainly! Through acquisition and growth, the company offers more options to its millions of customers. Correspondingly, note the change in the high concept that FedEx currently articulates: "Why fool around with anybody else?" In other words, the time frame may now be variable; however, the dependability is absolutely not.

Sometimes, You Clearly Have to Change

In the real world, sometimes we have to alter our business path. When I'm emphasizing clarity, I'm not suggesting that neither you nor your organization can make absolutely zero changes whatsoever to the strategies you develop as an outgrowth of this approach. Apple Computer added the iPod line and shortened its name to become Apple, Inc. Nothing wrong with that—especially when you are clear and precise that your focus is creating the most compelling, gotta own, high-tech devices on the planet.

We had to adjust one of our businesses at Obsidian—Pyramid Celebrity Coach—one that we were very clear about in terms of direction, but that was involved in a rapidly changing industry.

Pyramid leased many of the buses for celebrities and bands traveling to perform at concerts. (If you ever noticed Ozzy Osbourne on his bus during the television show in which he and his family starred, then you have seen a Pyramid Coach. He was one of our best customers.) We were extraordinarily clear about what the business entailed, and we had a pretty good high concept for a company transporting musicians: "You Sing—We'll Drive!" But what happens when the industry upon which you base your plans goes through a revolutionary upheaval?

The concert tours of many bands were supported by the recording companies that released their CDs—which, of course, meant that the income from the record labels was paying for their use of Pyramid Coaches. With the advent of downloads (legal and otherwise), and the distribution abilities native to iTunes and the Internet, these are not good times in the music business. As music attorney Peter Paterno, who represents Metallica and Dr. Dre said, "The labels have wonderful assets—they just can't make any money off them."[3]

When the industry that has been signing your checks—as the record labels were doing for us at Pyramid—is going through such a tremendous downturn, what do you do?

First, you understand and appreciate that there has been clarity about what you've *been*. Now, you need clarity about what you *will become*. We started examining nonvolatile industries and organizations that would also need our coaches. We found that university sports teams held great possibility. Although basketball and football teams would probably fly to their events, the golf, tennis, and soccer teams (among others) would need buses. No matter the economy, these student athletes would participate in their sport every year for an identical number of contests.

Another idea was to approach the Harrah's corporation, which was a client of my speaking business. I knew it was a company with outstanding management, starting with the chairman, Gary Loveman, who is originally from Obsidian's hometown of Indianapolis. We asked how the company was taking its high rollers to the riverboat casinos near Louisville and suburban Chicago.

"Why not do something unique for them?" we asked. "Put them in the same bus that the classic rock band Chicago used on some of its tours—or Ozzy—or major country music stars!"

At Pyramid Celebrity Coach, we are very clear about the fact that we are still in the celebrity coach business. Our new clarity, however, is that we partner with our corporate and university clients to make their customers *feel* like celebrities. The result? With fewer coaches—meaning less overhead and equipment worries—we are now more profitable with this division than we have ever been.

Success in Higher Education

Earlier, I mentioned my very close friend of many years Dr. Nido Qubein, now president of High Point University. Because of his success in the business world, Qubein was a member of the Board of Trustees of High Point University (HPU) at the time of his selection to become the institution's president. A member of the executive committee and board of directors of financial giant BB&T—and the chairman of the board of Great Harvest Bread Company—Qubein was a multimillionaire businessman, author, and speaker when he decided to make a significant difference for his alma mater.

One of the first aspects Qubein introduced to the institution was that the university had to become extraordinarily precise about its points of differentiation to begin to create clarity and distinction. Consider for a moment his competition for students: within just a few miles are nationally renowned institutions of higher learning such as Duke University, the University of North Carolina (UNC), and Wake Forest. Just a little farther down the road is North Carolina State University. How does a small college like HPU compete against UNC and the others?

First, Qubein created a high concept for his university upon assuming the duties of the presidency. It's a brilliant one that both students and parents love: "At High Point University, every student receives an extraordinary education in a fun environment with caring people." Who would not want to be a part of that?

Notice the depth of the statement as well. It requires the university to deliver on this promise to every student, not just those receiving scholarships or studying at an honors level. The education has to be extraordinary—not just the certification of a degree—and that's a pretty tall order when you consider the competitive atmosphere for the best students available. Although many of us may remember fun times during our college years, I doubt that a significant portion of us would state that our institution of higher learning was also committed to creating a "fun environment." Yet High Point University makes that pledge to its prospective students as well as those currently enrolled. Finally, HPU vows to students and their parents that the faculty and staff consist of "caring people." I imagine your experience in college was similar to mine. Some exceptional professors routinely displayed intense concern for their students, and some really didn't care whether students passed or failed. At High Point University, caring people create differentiation.

High Point will be an example we will visit again and examine its results. Remember, clarity is only the *first* cornerstone. Dr. Qubein and HPU will have to put several more stones in place to truly differentiate their institution and achieve distinction; however, this is a vitally important process to execute.

> ## If you don't begin the process, how can it possibly create results?

Remember, you cannot differentiate what you cannot define. Therefore, your goal is to be as precise as possible about who you are and what your organization is and what it is not. Be ready to fire prospects and customers who fail to fit your format.

Clarity is essential because those same customers asking, "Who are you?" will not present you with multiple opportunities to define yourself. After dealing with so many non-distinct organizations and professionals, they are vowing, they "won't get fooled again."

Now let's discover the second Cornerstone of Distinction: creativity!

Executive Summary

I. The First Cornerstone: Distinction is created by developing Clarity.

a. A question that most organizations and professionals cannot answer precisely is: *Who are you?*

b. Most cannot specifically define themselves or their organization.

  i. This does not mean the company name, product name, or a recitation of the mission statement.

  ii. It goes much deeper than that.

  iii. What is compelling? What will create a point of differentiation—and connect us to our customer?

c. Many organizations and professionals are so afraid of losing to their competitors that they strive to become "all things to almost all people."

  i. They believe it gives them more opportunity to attract customers.

  ii. Instead, it dilutes their differentiation, making them indistinguishable in the marketplace.

d. Excuses must stop!

  i. Even if your organization had the products of Apple, the people of Southwest, and the benefit packages of Starbucks, it wouldn't make a meaningful difference if you fail to create the clarity about what makes you distinctive in the market.

II. Not as easy as it seems!

a. Because the Cornerstone of Clarity means that you are precise about what you are, it also means you are exact about what you are *not*!

b. It is difficult for any organization or professional to "fire" a customer.

   i. Yet, attempting to be "all things to almost all people" is a major factor in diluting distinction.

      1. Starbucks admitted it "kind of lost its way" when it added everything from breakfast sandwiches to music to the product line.

      2. Be clear about what you are—and focus on your distinction.

   ii. If you, like the financial professionals cited in the text, cannot define precisely who and what you are, you are inviting the customers with the highest potential to go elsewhere.

      1. The prospects with the most promise are also the ones who seek specialists for their providers.

      2. Sending a message that "well, we are that, *too*," means that you will remain a "general practitioner" in a world that more highly rewards "specialists."

    c. The truth is that you have neither the time nor the energy to create highly distinctive customer experiences for a widely varied assembly of wildly diverse customers.

        i. Not even Wal-Mart sells everything to everybody!

III. The Process of Creating Clarity

    a. High Concept principle

        i. "Shark attack" makes you think of the movie, "Jaws."

        ii. "Bomb on a bus" makes you think of the movie, "Speed."

            1. These are high concepts from popular movies—and examples of the High Concept Principle created by Hollywood.

    b. It works in corporate America, as well.

        i. "Your pizza in thirty minutes" makes you think of Domino's.

    c. Individual professionals should create High Concept Statements, too.

IV. Creating your High Concept

    a. Consider these fundamental questions:

        i. What makes your business (or you) different . . . better . . . unique . . . from your competition?

       1. If you cannot answer these questions, neither can your employees or customers!

  b. Brainstorm with your colleagues

     i. What are the defining values of our organization?

     ii. What is espoused in our mission statement?

     iii. How could these points form the basis of a High Concept Statement?

     iv. How are they different from the aspects our competitors might use in their statements?

  c. Create a short, powerful, "grabbing" statement that interests and involves your audience of customers, colleagues, and prospects.

V. High Concepts are not just for the entire organization—every department within the organization requires one, as well.

  a. "We deposit the money that funds the dreams of thousands of families, including our own" (from the payroll department of a major corporation).

VI. Sometimes you have to change

  a. At times, organizations go through changes—or wish to initiate change—and, therefore, must alter their High Concept.

    i. Apple Computer, Inc. became just Apple, Inc. with the success of the iPod.

    ii. Pyramid Celebrity Coach changed from transporting music stars to their concerts to hauling college athletic teams and casino customers.

        1. The High Concept Statement changed from "You sing—we'll drive" (for music acts) to "Where our passengers are the real stars!" (for athletes and gamblers)

VII. Clarity is the starting point

    a. At High Point University, the new president, Dr. Nido Qubein, created a High Concept Statement as the starting point for the enhancements he wanted to create for the institution.

    b. "At High Point University, every student receives an extraordinary education in a fun environment with caring people."

        i. As we progress, we will observe how the actions of the institution were generated from the Clarity the new leader created.

VII. "You cannot differentiate what you cannot define."

    a. Start now. If you do not begin the process, it cannot create the results you desire.

Action Steps, Questions, and Ideas

- Who are you and your organization? How would you specifically define yourself to your customers? What are you all about? What will establish a connection with customers different from that of your competition? Please write down your answers, and do not list what you sell!

- If I asked one of your customers to describe you or your organization, what would he say? Would he be clear about who and what you are?

- How would you describe your target customers? What are they looking for? Who are they?

- When you describe yourself or your organization to customers—particularly if you relate your high concept to them—how is it different from the language that your competition would use?

Six

The Second Cornerstone: Creativity

This chapter will examine the importance of the Cornerstone of Creativity. You'll learn why it always follows Clarity in building distinction. This chapter will also present a three-step strategy for inspiring the innovation that will advance you beyond your competition. And, perhaps kindling a bit of controversy, I'll reveal why if you decide to forgo Creativity to merely follow well-publicized "best practices"—including the ones from a mega-bestselling business book—may not produce the results you desire

In *Corporate Creativity*, a leading book on the topic of creativity and business, authors Alan G. Robinson and Sam Sterm make the point that "creativity is essential to the workplace." And who would argue with that? Nevertheless, "in most companies, *potential creativity far exceeds creative performance.*"[1]

But is this surprising? Consider previous examples of non-differentiated professionals and organizations. Innovations are often focused on incremental improvements that do not require exceptional originality. And since many of us aren't really clear on who we are—or even whom we really seek to serve—the bar for inventiveness and imagination is set pretty low.

Author Bruce Airo addresses this in the magazine *Supervision*:

Creativity probably got a bad rap from many sources along the way. From our teachers on into adulthood, much of our influence has been to conform. Do the safe thing. Don't take risks. Do what everyone else is doing. We can view our lives as one long effort to toe the line. What a joy then when we can see another side. It's like a precious gift. Allowing and even promoting creativity is like that. Won't everything fall apart if everyone is going willy-nilly around doing their own independent thing? No, it doesn't mean that.[2]

Airo's article makes an important point. Often when I speak to organizations and managers about the importance of creativity within the process of developing differentiation, they act as if I am inviting chaos. He concludes, "Creativity is not equivalent to anarchy. It is different in an essential way. Anarchy is an absence of any structure. Creativity is an instinct to produce."[3]

I love the manner in which he defines the difference between these characteristics. He really explains why creativity is the second Cornerstone of Distinction.

Creativity Is Number Two

Visualize, if you will, a writer sitting down at her laptop with the "instinct to produce" and beginning to type. Could you even imagine that she would not know what the precise medium was going to be of the creative product she was producing? Obviously, the answer is no. In other words, when the most innovative artists in the world begin to develop from the fruits of their imagination, they are already crystal clear about the specific format for which they are writing.

She doesn't just start creating without already knowing whether she is developing a novel, screenplay, song, or poem. And no matter how wildly original her imagination, the artist still respects—at least to some degree—the restrictions of the format she has selected. Songs need music. Novels need words.

Yet herein lies much of the difficulty I've observed when organizations encourage their colleagues to "think outside the box." They somehow believe that creativity is stimulated *exclusive of restrictions*. But, as we see here, even the most creative artists understand that there are inherent limitations to any form. This is why developing creativity is the *second* Cornerstone of Distinction.

Creativity without clarity is devoid of distinction.

If we had attempted creative approaches with Pyramid Celebrity Coach before we revised and redefined our clarity, our efforts would have been counterproductive. By starting with clarity, the creativity we then applied had traction for the growth of our company.

"But I'm Not Creative!"

Before we spend too much time on the restrictions, let's examine how you can become more creative.

Countless authors offer ideas on how a professional or an organization can become more creative. Amazon lists nearly nine thousand books on creativity and business and almost two hundred thousand on creativity alone; it would seem that creativity is a difficult science—but not so. The codirector of Harvard University's Project Zero study of cognitive skills in the sciences and humanities, David N. Perkins, has said that creativity "has little to do with intelligence, talent or expertise. These may provide the raw horsepower for creative endeavors, but not the steering."[4] Everyone can do it.

Here are three ideas for stimulating and steering creativity that we will employ within the confines of the clarity we have already determined.

Creative Idea #1: Believe You Are Creative

One of my favorites sayings comes from the book *A Whack on the Side the Head* by Roger von Oech. He states that the key to being creative is simply *believing* that you are. That's it! So when someone protests, "But I'm not creative," the process immediately shuts down. The moment you tell yourself that you are devoid of creativity, you build a dam across the free flow of ideas. However, people who *believe* that they are creative will begin to generate ideas and concepts.

Creative Idea #2: Expose Yourself to Stimulus

Another question you must ask yourself is, "Am I being exposed to stimulus that will generate creativity?"

My good friend Randy Gage is a remarkable person who has risen from high school dropout to now earning acclaim as the "Millionaire Messiah" because his strategies have assisted so many of his clients in creating wealth. Randy has been quoted as saying:

> Creative people generally are self-motivated, independent, delighted by novelty, risk takers, tolerant of ambiguity, deeply involved in their work, avid readers, and world travelers. These characteristics provide creative people with a very rich diet of stimulation, variety and situations. They see the same thing handled in many different ways, so it opens up the mind to problem solving, lateral thinking and innovation.[5]

The person or organization desiring to enhance creativity must ask if there is systematic exposure to stimuli, such as Randy notes, that will build the essential spirit necessary to possess an open and productive mind. Ask yourself right now, "Have I put myself on 'a very rich diet of stimulation'?" If not, what action will you take to do so?

Creative Idea #3: Understand That Creativity Is Synergistic

If there is one word in the business vernacular that I feel has been overused, it is *synergy*. A greater-than-the-sum outcome resulting from the combination of two or more forces, we often lump people or departments together for no apparent motive, rationalizing that the move will create synergy. Organizations acquire a competitor and promise Wall Street that the merger will produce greater profits because of the new synergies. Most times, investors have been highly disappointed in the results. Nevertheless, if there is one place that this concept actually works, it is in the area of creativity.

For some mystical reason creativity is extraordinarily difficult in a vacuum. Ideas improve when shared with others. As George Endres, my close friend and formerly senior vice president for distribution of mutual funds for global financial giant Old Mutual, often reminds his colleagues, "*None* of us is as smart as *all* of us."

A brief article in *R&D* magazine informs us, "Collaborative technologies are vital to continual innovation. Sharing knowl-edge across a research group, organization or partnership sparks the breakthrough thinking necessary for the creation of new products and new ways of doing business."[6]

I can certainly state from personal experience that the concepts in this book and in my previous works have greatly benefited from sharing and discussing (sometimes almost to the point of arguing) them with friends who have alternative viewpoints.

A word of caution, however: be careful about *who* you choose to invite to become a part of your brainstorming group. We all know those people who brighten a room when they leave it! Don't bring creativity killers into your circle of synergy.

Stimulating Productive Creativity

If you are going to inspire productive creativity—the kind that can stimulate strategies that will have immediate positive impact on you and your organization—here are the three action steps you must take.

Step One: Drive It Down

Your first step is to rely upon your clarity to break down all customer interaction into the smallest units or steps possible.

Ask yourself this question: What is *every* point of contact that a customer has with me or my organization? Make an extremely detailed list.

During the Q & A session at a recent program in Portland,

Oregon, one member of the audience remarked that her company had "kind of forgotten that our product has to be installed." When I asked her for more insight into her problem, she continued, "We sell business communication systems that include everything from the actual telephone handsets to the service for telephone, wireless, Internet, and television. We have many wonderful advantages that our sales team works hard to communicate. Yet we never include the installers in this process. Therefore, we are getting frequent complaints that our technicians aren't creating positive experiences for our customers." She captured the essence of why it is so important to keep driving it down in Step One. Although many organizations are highly aware of the quality of communication between the salesperson and the customer, not nearly as many consider the impact of other representatives.

Now, the important question, what *happens* when customers are in contact with you? It's time to be very specific about the process. If you are like most organizations—or professionals—you aren't finding too much in the way of differentiation.

For example, if I rent a car, it seems to me that these are the basic points of contact:

1. Call the agency (or travel agent) and make a reservation or use the Web site of the agency or travel company to secure a reservation.

2. Travel to the agency location by its bus (at the airport) or by transportation I arrange (for local locations).

3. Enter the agency and proceed to the counter.

4. Process paperwork and provide payment for the reservation.

5. Obtain driving directions.

6. Proceed to the rental car.

7. Exit the lot through security.

8. Drive the rental car for the period of my contract with the agency.

9. Return the car to the agency location.

10. Determine the final cost of rental based upon contract agreement and fuel level.

11. Complete car check-in.

12. Depart agency.

Your next step should be to develop a similar list of the points of contact for your industry in general and your organization in particular. It's important that you drive this down to the most precise aspects possible.

Every point of contact with your customer provides an opportunity for distinction!

Consider the automobile manufacturer and dealer network for a moment. It takes years to engineer a new model of automobile. And as we have seen with the dramatic rise in the cost of gasoline, sometimes highly popular models—like SUVs—can fall out of favor rapidly. However, dealers could engage in new approaches to distinguish themselves from the competition immediately with creative improvements throughout the dealership.

Greeting each prospective customer with a concierge, offering no-haggle pricing, following up initial contact with telephone calls, maintaining ongoing contact with your sales consultant, staging wine-tasting events in the showroom with new car models, providing special driving programs associated with local racing events—perhaps even with NASCAR or IndyCar drivers—for sports car enthusiasts, using distinctly different advertising, and more are ways to create differentiation. All of this sounds fairly obvious, so one must ask, why aren't more dealers doing it?

It doesn't stop there, however. If I am an employee of the dealership, I must find creative strategies and techniques that will differentiate me from everyone else. The top salespeople get the best referrals; the rest get the crumbs. The top service technicians work on the best cars; the rest get the clunkers. These strategies for differentiation are vitally important for the company that wants its business to thrive *and* for the employee who wants her career to excel.

In their poignant book, *The Simple Truths of Service: Inspired by Johnny the Bagger,* Ken Blanchard and Barbara Glanz tell the story of a young grocery bagger with Down syndrome who, through his creativity, gives customers more than they expect. Therefore, he creates an enormous wave of enthusiasm and connection among his colleagues and his customers at the store where he works.[7]

I was with Ken Blanchard at a meeting in Lancaster, Pennsylvania, when he told the story of this creative young man who bagged groceries. He related that he had presented the same story to the staff of Petco Park, home stadium of baseball's San Diego Padres. At the end of a video for those employees prior to the grand opening of the park, he asked them, "Are you going to be a 'Johnny' tonight?"

Blanchard noted that throughout the baseball season, stadium managers and employees continued to ask one another, "Are *you* going to be a 'Johnny' tonight?" In the first summer that Petco Park was open, the team received more than seven thousand five hundred unsolicited letters from adoring fans who were compelled to take the time to write how they had been "blown away" (Blanchard's term) by the manner in which they were treated at the park.

The creativity of a grocery bagger not only brought distinction to his store, but also inspired others to do likewise. Why should you or I accept less from our organizations—or ourselves?

Step Two: Pick a Point

Now that you know that every one of these specific items is an opening for you to create space for your organization from your competition, the next step is to review each point of contact to ascertain where you can develop differentiation.

The greatest areas of differentiation that most customers observe are in logos and color schemes. We know that Hertz is yellow, Avis is red, and National is green in the rental car world. But does that have to be the case? Aren't there other meaningful ways to engage clients, ones that would help ensure repeat business? The last time I checked, a color on your sign would not accomplish that.

Enterprise Rent-A-Car has been clear about what it is—a company that rents automobiles. Yet when the company broke down the specific points of contact with customers, managers realized that at some point the renter has to obtain possession of the car. At other companies, customers must transport themselves to the rental locations, either at the airport or at a local office.

One of my favorite electronics retailers, Indianapolis-based H. H. Gregg, drove down its thinking regarding customer contact and recognized that many sales revolved around large products that required delivery. The customer's experience with delivery was one of the important points where contact was established and maintained on behalf of the organization.

Here's another example of driving it down, then picking a point: What ensues when customers pull into your parking lot? Have you even thought about it? Most businesses would say, "Well, good grief, they find a space and park!" Yet businesses that are dedicated to differentiate themselves will view such a basic action as an opportunity for distinction.

Joe Calloway is one of the nation's top professional speakers and a very close friend of mine. In his presentations, he often relates the story of Les Schwab Tires, a chain of about four hundred stores employing seven thousand people in the western United States.

I've heard Joe tell this story many times, and it never fails to elicit the audience response he desires. He says to the audience, "I'm thinking of a company based in the West that sells a commodity, yet they make it different." At this point, I've actually heard people call out, "Les Schwab!" But if Joe hasn't received his required response yet, he smiles and continues, "Let me give you a clue: tires." If they haven't already, the program participants familiar with Les Schwab shout the company's name. Then Joe asks the magic question, "What makes the company different?" Members of the audience then exclaim the answer.

Not only did Les Schwab and Enterprise and H. H. Gregg follow the first two steps of driving it down and picking a point, the company followed through with step three.

Step Three: Develop a Difference

Enterprise Rent-A-Car. In 1957 Jack Taylor launched Enterprise Rent-A-Car from the lower level of a St. Louis car dealership. Here's the story:

> Enterprise got its start by courting the airport passenger market. It could not afford to have space in the terminals, so their check-in facilities were located one or two blocks down the street. They countered this disadvantage by offering lower prices than Hertz

and Avis. Their advertising campaign consisted of a photograph of a handsome male, well dressed, and drinking a martini. The headline was, "Before I started using Enterprise Rent-A-Car, I lived with my mother." After they built some mass, they moved into the garage-rental market and switched their position to, "We'll pick you up." Their television commercials feature an automobile wrapped up like a gift package driving to the location of the person renting the car. The moral of the story is, regardless of how small your company is today, you can become a leader.[8]

By driving it down, picking a specific point—the manner in which the customer gets to the product—and *developing a difference,* Enterprise has grown into the largest rental car company in America.

Enterprise realized the creative opportunity for differentiation. If all the company did was to incrementally improve their airport locations against its competition at Hertz and Avis, Enterprise probably would have remained trapped by the Three Destroyers of Differentiation, and in all likelihood, the company would have collapsed. As it is, you can almost visualize the creative moment in a brainstorming meeting when someone said, "Wait a minute! What if we go *to* our customers? What if we take the car to them?" What differentiates Enterprise? You already know the answer: "At Enterprise—We Pick You Up." By being creative—within the boundaries of clarity—Enterprise developed a powerful point of distinction.

H. H. Gregg. I can clearly remember being a small tot and Aunt Kak (my young shorthand version of Katherine) taking me to a small appliance store on the north side of Indianapolis. As she shopped for a new refrigerator, this farm boy noted that the people from the big city were friendly and the selection seemed quite remarkable. I had never seen so many washing machines in one place in my life! We were at the original store of H. H. Gregg.

Fansy and H. H. Gregg started their store in 1955, offering washers, clothes dryers (and wringers), outdoor grills, and refrigerators like Aunt Kak was buying. Not long after, they added electronic products such as televisions. Today H. H. Gregg is an expanding group of about eighty-five stores in Alabama, Kentucky, Ohio, North Carolina, South Carolina, Tennessee, Florida, and Georgia—as well as its home in the Hoosier state. H. H. Gregg is opening stores, while competitors like Circuit City are closing locations. What has made the difference?

H. H. Gregg believes it has an advantage because of its knowledgeable employees and low-price guarantee. I respectfully disagree. I believe the edge in excellence stems from the fact that H. H. Gregg is clear about what it is, that it picked a point of opportunity for distinction, and that it developed a difference. Knowledgeable employees by themselves do not make a company distinct. It's not exactly as if competitors are seeking imbeciles; every organization says that it wants good people. And sure, Gregg's low-price guarantee means it will match the competition's price on equal items. But other major electronics retailers offer the same—or better—promise. So what makes the difference?

The distinguishing point about H. H. Gregg is its delivery to your home. If you purchase an item that is in stock (prior to a reasonable evening cut-off time), the company will deliver it to you the very same day! You can buy your new, enormous, flat-panel television in the morning and watch the big game on it in your home that night.

As Andrei Codrescu, publisher of the online journal *Exquisite Corpse*, said in an NPR commentary aired on *All Things Considered*: "We Americans don't like waiting. In the country of instant gratification, waiting is unbearable. So we don't usually wait. We make phone calls and set up meetings when the new batch of fries at McDonald's isn't out yet. We don't like lines."[9]

How true. After we decide on the specific flat panel TV, refrigerator, or washer-dryer combination that we are willing to spend our hard-earned money for, we want it *now*! And H. H. Gregg developed a point of distinction by delivering it to us the same day as our purchase.

Les Schwab Tires. After Joe Calloway asks the questions that move several in his audience to identify a tire retailer in the Pacific Northwest, he then inquires about the specific aspect that has developed differentiation for Les Schwab Tires. Those who have patronized this wonderful company yell, "They *run* to your car!" At this point, those of us who hail from other parts of the country sit and listen a bit stunned as Joe smiles, nods, and asks, "Can the rest of you believe it? When you pull in their lot, they run . . . not walk quickly, not jog. They run to your car to serve you!"

Les Schwab Tires calls this "Sudden Service," and the company's locations execute it to near perfection. Picture yourself needing a new set of tires and blocking out the better part of an afternoon to visit a few retailers in your area to get the best price. You know the size of tires your car must have; it's not as if you can negotiate a significant degree of variance on the requirements of this purchase as you might a car or a house. You are also aware that there are a few major, notable manufacturers, so your range of choices is certainly more limited than if you were deciding where to dine that evening. And the fact is that for most of us, we choose from the two or three brands that have better brand appeal than others (such as Firestone, Goodyear, or Michelin), or we don't care what they put on the car, just make it the cheapest on which we can get by (not enough perceived brand differentiation to influence our purchasing choice).

When you pull into the XYZ Tire Store, you walk in, stand in line, and are gruffly greeted by someone who, from the look of his hands, has obviously been mounting and balancing tires all day. You pull out the slip of paper noting the size of the tires you need, and he pounds a computer keyboard and says, "Buddy, here's what we got in stock." You note both the prices and his irritation when you say you are just checking around.

Next, at ABC Tire Store, you enter and find a clerk who

smugly asks you if you have an appointment. When you respond in the negative and say that you are just checking around, she pounds a computer keyboard and says, "Here's what we have in stock. Would you like an appointment for installation?" You reiterate that you're just checking and proceed to your third and final destination.

Now, imagine you've pulled into Les Schwab Tires. You see a clean, smartly dressed professional, wearing a neat, pressed uniform, run to your car to serve you with a smile. Do you perceive at this instant that Les Schwab Tires possesses a point of distinction? Obviously!

I suggest that even if the tires and prices are the same, which they may or may not be, you choose to do business with Les Schwab Tires because—as the Ebert Effect states—the company is different, and different is *superior*.

For an Organization

To achieve distinction, your organization does not have to make every attribute about what it does unique. Les Schwab Tires still mounts Goodyears (and others) on their customers' cars, just like the competition. That is not what makes the company distinct in its industry.

The differentiation comes from becoming highly creative in at least one single, solitary aspect of its connection with the customer. Such companies have found a point of distinction that creates distance between them and their competitors. And, let's face it, by being the first in their business to take this approach, they make it impossible for their competition to duplicate. If, all of a sudden, the employees at XYZ Tires started running for the cars, almost every prospective customer would think, *Wow. They must be in trouble. They're imitating—in fact, they're ripping off—Les Schwab.*

For the Individual Professional

For each of us on an individual level, the approach is exactly the same. What strategy can you implement that will create a point of distinction for you with your customers or within the organization—or both?

One manager I know works with her staff to set team goals, and when they are accomplished, the office has a "Film Friday." They'll pop some popcorn and watch the DVD of a movie on the big screen in the conference room. This manager is beloved by her colleagues. (How many times is business *really* like all of those football analogies some managers frequently employ? Seldom do we get to act as if we're crossing the goal line and spiking the ball. This manager creates that thrill of achievement for her team.) Imagine being the next manager in that office and attempting to discontinue the practice.

The sales professional who can find a specific point of differentiation in the manner in which he makes a call is the one who will find his customers more receptive to his calls—and his prospects more intrigued by what he has to say. *Motor*—a magazine for professionals in the auto repair business—reports that some salespeople at auto service shops are remarkably enhancing their sales by taking a creative step. They ask their customers if they would like to add a first-rate trailer hitch to their vehicles.

According to the article, "Many vehicles equipped with trailer hitches were never built to tow a significant amount of weight. This means they present opportunities such as more frequent preventive maintenance due to accelerated wear, as well as opportunities to sell and install other accessories, such as suspension upgrades, transmission coolers and a host of others." Then these same sales professionals follow up with these customers to promote service on the trailers that these customers are now hitching up to their cars. These "trailers eventually need maintenance on exterior lighting, suspension and brakes, tires, axle alignment, etc."[10]

Reflect on what that means for a moment: every single day in just about every community in the country auto repair sales professionals talk to customers. How difficult is it to ask a question to determine if they have ever considered hauling a boat? Or even the simpler, "Do you like to go fishing?"

Yes, It Is That Simple!

Running to your car, picking you up with a rental, asking if you tow a boat—it just sounds too simplistic to be a real factor in creating differentiation, doesn't it? Yet here is the remarkable aspect of creative distinction: it really is that simple!

One representative for a dairy company used to call on Mom and Dad at their grocery store and wear a small flower in his lapel. Every time, without fail, that flower was there. Mom ordered more from him because he was "classy." Dad always noted he was a "real gentleman." As a young and impartial observer, I didn't notice much that was different about his milk and cheese. However, something as simple—yet distinctive—as a flower in his lapel created a small bit of competitive space for him.

President Nido Qubein from High Point University expanded on the clarity of the high concept statement created by his team and started getting creative. Remember HPU's high concept? "At High Point University, every student receives an extraordinary education in a fun environment with caring people." The HPU team then developed innovative approaches for each segment of the high concept.

For example, how do you create the "fun environment" and deliver on that promise? One of the creative approaches was an HPU Ice Cream Truck. Between classes, the truck—often accompanied by HPU's mascot, Panther—offers treats to the students. Inside the Student Center is a traditional college dining hall as well as a real Starbucks, a Chick-fil-A, and more. In addition, every student has access to a—ready for this?—campus concierge! Each student can utilize the services—without additional cost—of a concierge for wake-up calls, dry cleaning, shopping, movie tickets, and any other appropriate service.

At the end of the day, the point of all of this has to be to improve the education that students receive and that parents support. A *Good Morning America* report broadcast on September 20, 2008 noted that because of all of these creative elements that are establishing a distinct student experience, HPU's students have a higher motivation for academic excellence than those at other, less innovative institutions. The results of these efforts? High Point University is now ranked by *U.S. News & World Report* in its "America's Best Colleges 2009" issue as the number one "up and coming" college among all comprehensive universities in the nation, and number five institution of all universities in the South.

Obama's Clear Message—Delivered Through Creativity

You can't have the clear message of being the "change" candidate and transmit that message in the same old manner as your competition. That's why the successful presidential campaign of Barack Obama employed new methods and integrated the second Cornerstone into their efforts: Creativity.

For example, the campaign successfully engaged supporters through an innovative approach to the social networking service called Twitter. This mini-blogging program enables members subscribing to this free service to interact by posting "tweets" (short text-based messages). Messages can either be broadcast to the over 3 million registered users, or restricted to people who have signed up as your friend, also known as your "followers." All Twitter subscribers generate a list of members to "follow," and the service tracks a list of those members who want to follow you.

By Election Day, the Obama campaign had 115,000 followers—the most of any account on the service. However, one of the keys to that success was that they were also *following* 119,000 members—and using the service to drive interested members to the Obama Web site, where they could learn more about the campaign, as well as make a financial contribution to the candidate. In addition, the ongoing status updates from the candidate (sent on an average of every other day for nineteen months) made those following feel both constantly and instantly connected in a manner never before seen in national politics.[11]

In addition, while the Obama team strategically decided that the youth vote was going to be vital to their success—something earlier campaigns from all the Kennedys to McGovern and others had done, as well—they also found highly creative approaches to reach them. Young adults playing the video game, "Burnout Paradise" on Xbox 360 would drive their virtual cars past a billboard noting that "Early Voting Has Begun: Obama 2008."

"I can confirm that the Obama campaign has paid for in-game advertising in Burnout," Holly Rockwood, director of corporate communications at the game's publisher, Electronic Arts (EA), told the Web site GigaOM. She noted that EA regularly allows ad placements in their online games. "Like most television, radio, and print outlets, we accept advertising from credible political candidates," she said.

What she did *not* note, however, was that, unlike television, radio, and print, no political candidate had previously been creative enough to tap into the large audience of young voters that an EA game like "Burnout" could deliver.[12]

Part of the creativity you need to bring to your clarity may be discovered and executed in the manner in which you stay connected to your customers.

An Exercise

Here is an exercise designed to develop your creativity regarding how you connect with colleagues and clients. Create a list of the primary approaches and strategies being used by other professionals that you have observed in your field. For example, if you are a manager, write down what other managers do as they provide leadership and direction to their people. If you are a salesperson, write down the sales approaches and techniques that are common in your industry.

My suggestion is to invest significant time in this exercise. You need to make a fairly complete list of the standard practices in your profession and for your position. Now review and consider all of the approaches on your paper. Carefully examine them.

Then *don't do them!*

This idea may sound one-dimensional at first. If you really evaluate this little exercise, however, I believe you will begin to understand why it is at the heart of creativity. And I realize that I'm overstating the case a bit here: if some of the approaches are moral absolutes—upholding equality, diversity, and respect for individuals and others—you should obviously continue their application.

The main point I want you to consider is that imitation usually generates neither passion nor distinction. If you are copying from others—even if you are imitating the best—you are propagating a "me too" approach that will continue to cast you adrift on the sea of sameness.

Perhaps It's Best Not to Pursue Best Practices

In the past several years, I have met too many "best practice junkies." You may have worked for—or with—one of these types. They are always on the lookout for the next set of approaches they can imitate. They are practically groupies of organizations which have become so dominant that they are almost business clichés—Starbucks, Southwest, Apple, and Nordstrom, for example—and use their practices as their business Bible. They become so enthralled with a creative best practice from another organization that they often neglect to evaluate whether that approach is applicable for *their* situation. Of course, for many professionals, it's much easier to imitate someone else's best practices than to creatively develop their own.

Back in September 1993, Dr. Jac Fitz-enz, founder of the Saratoga Institute in Santa Clara, California, illuminated some of the primary problems with best practices in the professional journal *Human Resource Planning*. "Many business articles focused on 'best practice' firms result in misleading conclusions regarding business success," Dr. Fitz-enz stated.

Let's look at some of the problem areas, starting with the basics. For example: what does "best" mean? This is a highly subjective, nonspecific question. Who says what's best? On what basis do they say it's best? For whom is it best? In what way is it best? In searching for answers, we may fall victim to such fallacies as the "halo effect." We read about Company X, and the article says they're absolutely great at such and so. And it's true; they are. But, in the absence of a sufficiently sharp, specific focus, the reader may buy into the notion that they're great at everything. Nobody is.

What he is saying supports—from organizational and personal perspectives—our approach in putting clarity before creativity. Pick your specific focus and be abundantly clear about that first. Then develop creative approaches that build distinction in precisely defined areas. We already know that no organization—and no professional—is going to be great at everything. Dr. Fitz-enz continued,

Another dangerous pitfall is the "small sample extension." Somebody looks at a few companies—and extrapolates the outcomes to *infinity*. Not only is a "best practice" subjective—it's transitory.

It changes faster than dress styles. What was best last month may not be best today. In fact, by the time you read about it, it may be passé. It may even have gone from being right to being *downright wrong.*[13]

"Good to . . . Mediocre"?

Now here is where I might get into trouble. Jim Collins' book *Good to Great* is a mega-best seller.[14] It is a "must read" in the business community, and its concepts are discussed ad nauseum at conferences, seminars, and conventions—its teaching accepted as gospel at many organizations. While I am appreciative of his research and impressed by his extraordinary accomplishments, I nevertheless believe that several of the significant points selected by Collins to exemplify what makes a company "great" are simply incorrect. This, I would suggest, renders some of the book's business principles unhelpful for organizations and individuals attempting to attain differentiation.

In the book, Collins selects eleven companies by means of statistical models and extensive research. One is Circuit City, now a bankrupt company dying a slow death because it evidently did not know how to differentiate from a competitor such as Best Buy. An article on Forbes.com dated February 26, 2008 read:

Circuit City reported a $207 million loss in its fiscal third quarter, and anticipates a "modest loss" in the fourth quarter, the period that included the bulk of the crucial holiday-shopping season. The company has floundered after experiencing a devastating third quarter loss, reported last December 21, of $207.3 million. The losses came after Circuit City fired 3,400 experienced workers to replace them with lower-waged workers.[15]

That meant customers of this "great" company had a difficult time during the Christmas rush finding employees who knew what they were doing and could answer questions. This led to Circuit City announcing later in 2008 that they were closing about twenty percent of their stores and firing thousands of additional workers. "The weakened environment has resulted in a slowdown of consumer spending," said James A. Marcum, vice chairman and acting president and CEO. However, I would suggest the primary problem *isn't* the economy—it's the inability of the "great" Circuit City to create differentiation.

Don Reisinger, columnist for C-net News, explains it this way:

Why is it so hard for everyone discussing Circuit City's Chapter 11 filing and New York Stock Exchange stock suspension to tell the world what really happened with this company?

No, Circuit City isn't dying because of the credit crunch, and there's no way we can blame its demise on the preferential treatment competitors like Best Buy are receiving. And we certainly can't blame it on the online-retail industry.

Knowing that Circuit City's executives over the past eight years have single-handedly ruined any prospect for growth, thanks to questionable decisions and poor management of company assets, the current team of executives wants to blame everyone else but themselves.

The numbers and the financial data speak for themselves; the only reason Circuit City is in ruin today is because of the company's executives. After all, Best Buy is competing in the same environment, and that company has performed extremely well. Why couldn't the sector's most prominent company from years ago have done the same?

It's unfortunate, but there's no saving Circuit City now. The game is over, and the retailer has lost. [16]

Yet, in "Good to Great," Collins praises Circuit City's then-CEO not only for his corporate approach and vision, but also for how he selected and managed the members of his team.

Things have also fared poorly at some of the other *Good to Great* companies. While it is an ethical matter, and not one based upon sheer economics and management, it would be highly difficult for me to ever proclaim Philip Morris as a "great" company. When the result of extended use of your product results in the illness or death of your best customers, how can it be argued that the company is "great"? However, Collins reported that his selection "stuck much closer to the tobacco business, in large part because they loved that business." He stated he was "surprised" by their "passion" and notes an interview with a board member who "proudly puffed away" during their conversation. I just disagree. When your product has been proven to be a legitimate threat to kill your customers, you are disqualified in my book from greatness.

Walgreens' stock price has shrunk while supposedly "non-Great" CVS has grown. While *Good to Great* touted Walgreens in 2001 as the winner over CVS—and states that "great companies, for the most part, have always been great"—by 2008, Walgreens was under intense pressure from shareholders to match the results of its major competitor. "Even the best of companies at times have to change their business model," said Gregory Wasson, Walgreens president and chief operating officer. [17]

Gillette was acquired by Proctor & Gamble. Pitney Bowes—with a core product helping customers deliver junk mail—has only recently decided, after 85 acquisitions, that the company is going to "re-brand" itself and consider a "whole brand" philosophy. Perhaps the best thing about *Good to Great* was the title. Or, as above, *best practices aren't always best*.

In an interview, business guru Tom Peters stated that the

companies that Jim calls great have performed well. I wouldn't deny that for a minute but they haven't led anybody anywhere. I don't give a damn whether Microsoft is around 50 years from now. Microsoft set the agenda in the world's most important industry at a critical period of time, and that to me is leadership, not the fact that you are able to stay alive until your beard is 200 feet long. [18]

In the book, Collins also proclaims, "In fact, leaders of companies that go from good to great start not with 'where' but with 'who.' They start by getting the right people on the bus, the wrong people off the bus, and the right people in the right seats."[19]

Really? Here's my question: *Would you get on a bus if you did not know where it was going?*

And note one of the primary corporate examples that the book employed to exemplify the "right people on the bus"—financial giant Fannie Mae! Even well before the September 7, 2008 move by the Federal Housing Finance Agency to place Fannie Mae under federal conservatorship, here was an organization the *Washington Post* reported in 2004 that had "maintained a corporate culture that emphasized stable earnings at *the expense of accurate financial disclosures*." (emphasis added)[20] Following the federal takeover, the Fannie Mae Web site reported that its "Board of Directors no longer has the power or duty to manage, direct or oversee the business and affairs of Fannie Mae." The CEO and CFO of Fannie Mae have resigned, and the *Wall Street Journal* reported in June 2008 that two former CEO's received their personal home loans at below market rates from Countrywide Financial—when Fannie Mae was the biggest purchaser of Countrywide's mortgages. When you examine the financial debacle in the mortgage industry that precipitated today's economic crisis, any reasonable observer has to include this organization as one of the culprits. So, I ask you—*these* are the "right people" in the "right seats"?

On another front my colleague, friend, and fellow Speakers

Roundtable member Charlie Plumb was a prisoner of war in North Vietnam for nearly six years. He has stated on many occasions that the section in *Good to Great* regarding the assertion of Admiral James Stockdale that the "optimists" were the ones who didn't make it out was the opinion of only *one* P.O.W.— Stockdale himself. Called in the book, "The Stockdale Paradox," it says, "You must never confuse faith that you will prevail in the end—which you can never afford to lose—with the discipline to confront the most brutal facts of your current reality, whatever they might be."

However, as Plumb related to me, the problem is that it seems to him that the text is derisive of those who were the optimists—a category in which Plumb squarely places himself.

Charlie Plumb, author of *I'm No Hero*, states that it is impossible to make the choice to become an optimist—which the Encarta Dictionary defines as "somebody who tends to feel hopeful and positive about future outcomes"—without realistically understanding the set of circumstances about which you are optimistic. True optimists confront the facts and *choose* to feel hopeful, and according to Plumb, were the ones who dealt with the extreme challenges the P.O.W.'s faced most productively. Pessimists confronted the same set of facts, and came to a less positive attitude.

My point is this: there are a myriad of concepts presented by a multitude of business books. Whether the point is "The Stockdale Paradox" or getting the "right people on the bus," the fact remains that no one has truly defined a formula that can always make a company "great." I promise there is no silver bullet located in this text.

However, my research and my personal experience has convinced me that organizations that clearly and creatively seek to differentiate—and raise their performance to a level that creates distinction—will naturally become superior to inconspicuous competitors.

On the day I am writing this, Starbucks announced lower-than-expected earnings, and the aforementioned chairman, Howard Schultz, cautioned that the company was entering a difficult period. Starbucks sales have fallen, as has store traffic. "The wheels have really come off of this train," RBC Capital Markets analyst Larry Miller told Reuters, noting his surprise at the warning. "It's amazing how fast business has derailed. If sales are down mid-single digits, that is a rapid erosion."

Some of the differentiated companies identified in this book may still encounter difficult times. It's quite possible that the executives and managers I tout here will not deliver the results that their colleagues or shareholders anticipate.

So if a top-flight, creative, and differentiated company like Starbucks or like the companies in *Good to Great* can encounter challenges, why should you expend significant effort to become distinct?

It is true, you may very well take a tumble in difficult times. Nevertheless, if you have made the effort to build differentiation, you have begun a defense against being knocked out. When the economy tightens and the market shrinks, a differentiated company may not have gross earnings or net profits as substantial as before. Individual professionals—especially those with compensation tied to commissions or revenue—may experience a considerable decline in income. Yet in many situations, their competitors may be going out of business entirely. Just ask yourself how much lower your company could go if it wasn't differentiated? *Differentiation is like a vaccine for your career and your company.*

There's No Right Way

Starbucks, like Circuit City, suggests that its problem is based on a tightening economy. However, in the case of the coffee retailer, store sales have declined most in the areas hardest hit by economic volatility, suggesting validity to their theory. Initial research indicates that people are not dumping Starbucks to drink coffee someplace else. People just aren't spending as much on lattes when gasoline costs around four dollars a gallon (at this writing). And, while Starbucks reported a 97 percent drop in profit in Third Quarter 2008, that figure was primarily due to charges associated with restructuring. What's often overlooked is that—even with the challenging economy in 2008—Starbucks brought in $10.4 billion, a ten percent increase over 2007![21]

I would be willing to place my bet on Starbucks—when average consumers find more change in their pockets in a better economic cycle, they will enhance their orders from a tall to a grande or vente.

You do not need to change everything about how you do business to create distinction. Start by walking through your list of points of contact with customers, reframing and redefining how you perceive each moment of interaction. From these new perspectives, you can then begin to create specific points of differentiation with your customers. By developing your professional laundry list from the exercise—and recognizing that if these practices are the industry standard, then they will almost always fail to create distinction for you—you are taking an important first step in disciplining yourself as a professional to develop differentiated methods and tactics. Different is not just good, different is *better*.

It Shouldn't Be a Secret

All the creativity in the world won't do you or your organization any good if you keep your new, compelling ideas a secret. It is time to shine! You now have a powerful story to tell. The next chapter will focus on why it is so important to tell it, and outline how to do that in today's world.

Executive Summary

I. The second of the Four Cornerstones of Distinction is: Creativity

    a. In most companies, the creative potential far exceeds creative performance.

        i. Most of us truly believe we are not creative.

    b. Creativity is an "instinct to produce."

        i. Our goal is to be creative, so we can produce efforts that create distinction.

II. Creativity must be second—following Clarity.

    a. Creativity without Clarity is devoid of distinction.

        i. Even the most creative artists respect the baseline of restrictions of the format they have selected.

            1. Novels require words; Songs require music

        ii. Therefore, the creativity we are going to generate will always be grounded within the clarity we have developed from the first Cornerstone.

III. Three steps to Creativity

    a. Believe you are creative

        i. Once you believe you aren't creative, you stop attempting originality

        ii. The first step to creativity is simply believing you are creative

    b. Expose yourself to stimulus

      i. Creative people expose themselves to stimulating—and even controversial—thoughts from books, movies, and other forms of art.

      ii. They open up their mind to innovation by building the spirit necessary to create.

  c. Understand that creativity is synergistic.

      i. *"None* of us is as smart as *all* of us."

      ii. Brainstorm with other bright, stimulating people to grow creativity through synergy.

IV. Stimulating productive creativity

  a. Drive it down

      i. Break down the points of contact between your organization (or you) and your customer.

      ii. *Each* of these points provides an opportunity for you to creatively differentiate yourself.

  b. Pick a point

      i. Choose one of these specific points of contact and practice creativity.

         1. Enterprise Rental Car created distinction by picking the point of how their customers acquired the rental car.

  c. Develop a difference

      i. Positively exploit that area you have selected

    1. Enterprises exploited the point by differentiating themselves from their competitors by picking up their customers, instead of having them go to the rental car location.

       a. "At Enterprise, we pick you up!"

    2. Other examples include H.H. Gregg's same day delivery of appliances, and Les Schwab Tires's "sudden service" of running to a customer's car.

V. Creativity that is congruent with your Clarity

  a. High Point University developed extraordinary Creativity based upon the Clarity described earlier.

    i. For example, the "fun environment" promised was achieved with a campus truck of ice cream and bottled water for students between classes.

      1. And, a campus concierge that handles wake-up calls, dinner reservations, and dry cleaning for students.

  b. The result is that HPU was named by "U.S. News & World Report" as the "number one up and coming" institution of higher learning in the nation.

VI. "Best practices" aren't always "best"

  a. Your creativity is vital. Following trends, often called "best practices," can have unintended consequences.

    i. Some become so enthralled with what marquee companies like Starbucks and Apple are doing, they believe doing the same thing will have a similar effect upon their organization or career.

b. The dangerous "small sample extension"

    i. Research proves that extrapolating these best practice outcomes beyond their scope in this hyper-changing marketplace often fails to produce the desired results.

c. The fallacies of "Good to Great"

    i. Jim Collins's bestseller selected eleven "great" companies:

        1. Of them, Circuit City is now in bankruptcy,

        2. Gillette was acquired by a "non-Great" company,

        3. Phillip Morris' products can cause death or illness to its best customers,

        4. Fannie Mae is at the center of the nation's financial and housing market collapse,

        5. And Walgreen's is making significant changes because of the larger success of its "non-Great" competitor, CVS.

    ii. "The people on the bus are more important than where the bus is going" is clearly wrong!

    1. Would YOU get on a bus if you didn't know where it was going?

    2. High performers respond to clear and creative visions!

VII. Distinction is the ONLY approach that generates greatness with longevity

  a. While some of the companies touted in this book, or others that have developed differentiation, may achieve lesser results depending upon the market or choices by their leaders, true distinction is like a vaccine for your career and your company.

  b. Organizations and professionals that clearly and creatively seek to differentiate themselves—and raise their performance to the level that creates distinction—will naturally become superior to inconspicuous competitors.

    i. There is no single "right way" to do business.

    ii. Any "guru" that attempts to define it is simply misleading the reader.

    iii. However, those professionals and organizations that follow the Four Cornerstones will naturally find themselves creating space from the pack.

      1. And, as we learned earlier from the Ebert Effect, "different IS better."

Action Steps, Questions, and Ideas

- What is every point of contact that a customer has with you or your organization? Make an extremely detailed listing.

- Select one of these points of contact. Then create five innovative strategies for enhancing the quality of the contact with your customer at that stage.

- Select one challenge your organization faces in creating distinction in the marketplace. Then attempt to redefine the challenge from another perspective. Write down your new approach to an old problem.

Seven

The Third Cornerstone: Communication

I was about to give a presentation for one of my best clients, Old Mutual, at the Doubletree Hotel in Overland Park, Kansas. As I was entering our meeting room, the banner of another organization holding a conference across the hall stopped me in my tracks. I looked at it with amazement. I tapped an Old Mutual insurance executive on the shoulder, pointed out the poster, and said, "That may be the most foolish phrase I have ever seen at a business meeting."

The theme of the other organization's conference was "Sales Cure Everything!"

I could not believe the organization's ignorance and the erroneous information it was communicating to its team. *Sales* do not cure everything—not by a long shot!

If your organization isn't serving your customers well, do more sales cure that problem? Of course not.

If your company cannot retain good employees because it lacks the clarity necessary to create distinction, do more sales cure that? Absolutely not.

If you cannot make your product stand out in the marketplace, and you slice your price—selling more, *but earning significantly less*—does that cure everything for you and your organization? You know it doesn't.

If you fail to communicate what your organization is about, what it stands for—or what makes you clearly compelling individually as a professional—will hawking more of your stuff cause your challenges in communication to evaporate? Please don't deceive yourself into thinking that it might.

What Sales Do Accomplish

Here's what sales do: If you are a commission-based professional enduring a slow month, more sales make the pain of that period easier to handle. If you are judged on revenue you generate, more sales will temporarily prevent your managers from calling you on the carpet. If you lead a public company, more sales may avert your share price from falling for a bit. If you own a small business, more sales may briefly keep your banker at bay. However, while more sales may *ease the symptoms* of a current situation or keep it on life support, more sales definitely do not *cure* anything.

Sales—perhaps—*extend* everything. Sales don't alleviate your problems but may mean you can suffer them a while longer.

Differentiation and Distinction Cure What Ails You

Building distinction is the strategy that takes an ailing organization or career and gets it back on its feet and in the race. *Differentiation* has taken organizations from being in corporate intensive care to winning the business equivalent of the Olympic gold. And differentiation and the resulting personal and organizational distinction just do not happen without compelling communication.

What would have happened if, during the darkest days at Harley-Davidson—immediately after the thirteen senior executives had purchased the company back from AMF in 1981—those leaders had communicated to their team this message: "Ladies and gentlemen, just focus on sales. *Sales cure everything*"?

Their company was in an incredibly difficult situation. Product quality had become a joke, and the Super Glide bike had a horrible reputation. Harley dealers and their customers—

ignored and abused by the previous regime—were now bolting to other manufacturers. Instead of saying "sales cure everything," the Harley executives announced that "The Eagle Soars Alone" and dedicated themselves and their company to becoming the distinct leader in their market by reconnecting and intensely communicating with their current customers and making a compelling case for prospects. You know how that story turned out, right?

And therein lies the most important point. Lots of companies seek a superior position in the marketplace, just as Harley aspired to claim. However, you remember Harley *not* because you happen to recall the price of the acquisition paid to the former owner by the management team. Nor do most of us specifically remember what Harley shares were trading for when it returned as a public company a few years later, compared to its current valuation.

What we remember is the *story* that Harley communicated.

To more thoroughly understand why, you have to master the third Cornerstone of Distinction—*communication*.

This chapter examines how you can exchange your information with customers in a manner that is compelling and engaging. It will show you why creating emotional impact is vitally important in today's culture, how to link with clients through the "power of story," and present a simple "three-act" structure for constructing and conveying your narrative so that it builds distinction for you in the marketplace.

Information or Connection?

You and your organization probably have access to reams of data about what your customers are purchasing and why. If you are an entrepreneur with a small business, you likely belong to a trade association that can offer you a similar quantity of research. The problem is that only a fraction of these assessments will provide real insight into how you can take your clarity—now combined with creativity toward building unique and highly specific points of differentiation between you and your competitors—and turn that into communication that truly *connects* with your customers and prospects.

We tend to abdicate our aspirations of profound customer rapport solely to companies that create significant sensory responses—such as Harley-Davidson and other previously mentioned organizations such as Apple. Most of us in business stand amazed at the bond and loyalty inspired by those select few. Harley-Davidson customers are willing to tattoo its logo on their bodies! That is a connection almost beyond description! And— not coincidentally—many of us can tell the stories of these companies. We know how Harley came back from the brink of extinction. We know about the return of Steve Jobs to the company he helped found in a garage, about Herb Kelleher creating an airline on a cocktail napkin, and about Fred Smith writing a master's thesis about the company he wanted to establish. We are enthralled by their stories, but we tend to dismiss our own.

That, in my opinion, is a big mistake. But it would be a profound blunder to presume that only a select few companies possess either the history or the ability to engender stories written about them that can create a connection with customers and prospects. Every organization and every professional have a compelling story. For most of us, though, the problem is the story is still waiting to be told.

Everyone loves a story. Legendary computer scientist Alan Kay, formerly of Disney and now head of the Viewpoints Research Institute, has said: "Why was Solomon recognized as the wisest man in the world? Because he knew more stories—proverbs—than anyone else. Scratch the surface in a typical boardroom and we're all just cavemen with briefcases, hungry for a wise person to tell us stories."[1] I saw this firsthand when I was asked to return to my hometown of Crothersville and give a lecture for school teachers and administrators.

I have to admit that well before the program even started I was already feeling scared to death. Sitting in the front row was one of my former teachers! Part of the problem I experienced was caused by my memories of the tremendous crush that I had during my elementary school years on this then-cute, petite, very young teacher. On my return home, I naturally looked forward to seeing her again. However, the image in my mind of her was of the way she looked when I was in the third grade. Imagine my shock to see her now—sixty-two years old—and noticing that her stretch pants had no choice! Of course, she was just as shocked . . . standing in front of her was not the skinny, bespectacled eight-year-old kid with the "burr" haircut of her memories. It was a mid-forties guy with a mustache and a bit of a potbelly!

Being more than just a little nervous, I decided to start my presentation with a very standard question that many speakers and authors ask to begin a lecture to teachers. "Let's start by having you tell me," I said, "what you believe is the biggest problem for educators in today's world."

I thought I knew the answers these teachers were going to give. Naturally, their biggest problems were going to be: 1) disciplining the students, 2) encouraging the involvement of parents, 3) dealing with change and, 4) funding challenges in education.

Imagine my surprise when my former teacher raised her hand and declared, "Scott, I believe the biggest problem in education today is 'Sesame Street.'" I immediately responded with a profound, "Huh?"

Calmly, my former educator asked me, "Scott, who taught you your ABCs?"

I answered truthfully, "Well, my mother and my grandmother."

"Of course," she said. "However, for the last thirty years, young people have been taught their ABCs by Big Bird, and Bert and Ernie. That means they arrive on the steps of this school for their very first day of formal instruction expecting to be entertained as they are educated."

"Wow!" I thought. Then I realized, my elementary school teacher was still teaching me.

In this age when most of us grew up learning our ABCs from Big Bird and Cookie Monster rather than the disciplined repetition of a former time, our fervent desire for a wise person or distinct organization to tell us stories continues to expand. We are hungry for stories.

The Powerful Story of a Very-Senior Citizen

Throughout Barack Obama's successful presidential campaign, he relied on compelling stories to connect with his audiences. However, there is no better example than a story he related to the hundreds of thousands in Grant Park in Chicago (and the millions watching globally) on election night. Even though he received over 65,000,000 votes that historic day, the new president-elect concentrated on the story of just one solitary voter.

This election had many firsts and many stories that will be told for generations. But one that's on my mind tonight is about a woman who cast her ballot in Atlanta. She's a lot like the millions of others who stood in line to make their voice heard in this election except for one thing—Ann Nixon Cooper is 106 years old.

She was born just a generation past slavery; a time when there were no cars on the road or planes in the sky; when someone like her couldn't vote for two reasons—because she was a woman and because of the color of her skin.

And tonight, I think about all that she's seen throughout her century in America—the heartache and the hope; the struggle and the progress; the times we were told that we can't, and the people who pressed on with that American creed: Yes, we can.

At a time when women's voices were silenced and their hopes dismissed, she lived to see them stand up and speak out and reach for the ballot. Yes, we can.

When there was despair in the dust bowl and depression across the land, she saw a nation conquer fear itself with a New Deal, new jobs and a new sense of common purpose. Yes, we can.

When the bombs fell on our harbor and tyranny threatened the world, she was there to witness a generation rise to greatness and a democracy was saved. Yes, we can.

She was there for the buses in Montgomery, the hoses in Birmingham, a bridge in Selma, and a preacher from Atlanta who told a people that "we shall overcome". Yes, we can.

A man touched down on the Moon, a wall came down in Berlin, a world was connected by our own science and imagination. And this year, in this election, she touched her finger to a screen, and cast her vote, because after 106 years in America, through the best of times and the darkest of hours, she knows how America can change. Yes, we can.[4]

Note that Barack Obama *could* have said, "Look, in this country we've had slavery, depression, wars, moon landings, and a whole lot more. This night is going to go down in history, too.

Now . . . let's get to work." However, viewing these monumental events through the eyes of a woman who earlier in her life could not even cast a ballot because of her race, then because of her gender, presents all of these chapters of our nation's history in a more personal—and powerful—dimension.

Understanding Story

A significant voice on the subject of the power of stories and myth is Joseph Campbell. His work is one of the most significant texts available on how to craft compelling, emotionally connecting stories. Campbell's work from the 1940s, *The Hero with a Thousand Faces*, has influenced generations of storytellers, including *Star Wars* creator George Lucas, who stated that his blockbuster series of films was shaped by this approach.[2]

One of Campbell's main points is that for a story to be compelling, the hero cannot begin the narrative as the winner. In other words, a story about your professional or personal efforts—or about the growth and development of your organization—cannot begin with your success. The Harley-Davidson story is compelling in great part because the company was on the brink of disaster. Apple started in the garage, *not* as a darling of Wall Street, and the return of Steve Jobs as the company was on the brink of extinction makes the story even more gripping.

Campbell said, "A hero is someone who has given his or her life to something bigger than oneself."[3] Only through trials and tribulations—being tested and defeated and then rising up to conquer—do we really become heroes.

In Homer's *Odyssey*, Ulysses is not a hero at the beginning of the book. It is through facing his trials and challenges that he *becomes* one. In the New Testament one way in which his followers recognized Jesus as divine was through his ability to endure and resist varied forms and incarnations of temptation. The impact of *The Odyssey* or the New Testament would be greatly diminished without the tribulations their heroes successfully overcome.

We are story junkies. We get hooked on good stories. They can be scripted, as the soap operas demonstrate before millions of viewers daily. They can be reality based, as *Survivor* and the glut of imitators that have followed in the many years since are clearly proving. Or they can even be grounded in the business world.

The Benefits of Story

Mary E. Boyce, professor in the Department of Management and Business at Whitehead College, University of Redlands, California, wrote in the *Journal of Organizational Change*:

> Shared storytelling has a number of applications that warrant consideration by organizational members, managers, and practitioners. These are:

(a) Expressing the organizational experience of members or clients;

(b) Confirming the shared experiences and shared meaning of organizational members and groups within the organization;

(c) Orienting and socializing new organizational members;

(d) Amending and altering the organizational reality;

(e) Developing, sharpening, and renewing the sense of purpose held by organizational members;

(f) Preparing a group (or groups) for planning, implementing plans, and decision making in line with shared purposes; and,

(g) Co-creating vision and strategy.[5]

Boyce's article addresses the benefits of communication through story from an internal organizational perspective. I suggest that the power of story must also be applied on the exterior so that communication through a compelling and powerful story creates a persuasive bond between you and your customers, clients, and prospects. To see how influential this can become, let's look at a story about the Macintosh computers from Apple.

Your Customers, Your Sales Force

The cover story from *Business Week* in mid-May 2008, written by Peter Burrows, discloses that there is a large—and rapidly growing—number of employees in thousands of companies who request Apple's Mac on the job rather than the standard-issue Windows-based machines.

According to Burrows, one reason that Macs are not even more prevalent in the corporate world is that Apple has no sales force dedicated to marketing its products to businesses as the competition at Dell and HP does, for example. Yet because the millions of dedicated fans in the "cult of Mac" (of which I, too, am a proud member!) know the story and are enthusiastic about retelling it; Apple's customers have become a de facto sales team for the company.

"Soon after Michele Goins became chief information officer at Juniper Networks in February, she decided to respond to the growing chorus of Mac lovers among the networking company's 6,100 employees. For years, many had used Apple's computers at home and clamored for them in the office as well," Burrows writes. "So she launched a test, letting 600 Juniper staffers use Macs instead of the standard-issue PCs that run Microsoft's Windows operating system. As long as the extra support costs aren't too high, she plans to open the floodgates. 'If we opened it up today, I think 25 percent of our employees would choose Macs,' she says."

Burrows continues:

Funny thing is she [Goins] has *never received a single sales call* from Apple. . . . It's a people's revolution, of sorts, with workers increasingly pressing their employers to let them use Macs in the office. . . . Mark Slaga, chief information officer of Dimension

Data, a large computer services firm based in suburban Johannesburg, says he has received 25 e-mails recently from employees who want permission to use Macs at work. So far he has refused, because he doesn't want to hire people to provide Mac tech support, but "it'll happen someday," he concedes. *"Steve Jobs doesn't need a sales force because he already has one: employees like the ones in my company."*[6]

Wouldn't you like it if your customers also became a sort of voluntary sales force? That can occur only if your clients are able to communicate your story for you. And let's face it, if you aren't telling your story, you can't expect *them* to do so!

Again, it would be easy to dismiss this as an impossible phenomenon to duplicate without a hip product like the iPhone or MacBook Air, but that would be an incorrect assumption. It isn't difficult to find many other companies creating this kind of enthusiasm in their customers. From Levenger's, for fountain pens and upscale tools for readers, to Carl Nielsen, my car salesman at Dreyer & Reinbold BMW in Indianapolis, I have often been an advocate of large and small organizations and of individual professionals as well—and so have you! The unifying elements among all of these people and companies are that they are differentiated and they have a distinct story to tell—one that they have told me and that I have repeated.

My hope is that the discussion in this chapter is moving you toward understanding the importance of telling your story. The companies I've mentioned are all market leaders. Individuals like Carl Nielsen are top performers. They have attained distinction not only in their respective industries, but also throughout the entire marketplace. And they all tell their story. I call this a *clue*!

Customers seek that magical quality of *distinction*! As we have already discovered, distinction is developed by organizations and professionals that first develop clarity about what they are—followed by creativity in their approach—then *communicate* their story in a compelling manner. It is no coincidence that these organizations that we are tired of hearing about—Southwest, Starbucks, Apple, and so forth—are the ones that most frequently tell their stories in a precise and compelling manner. Yet why is it so difficult to find other examples? I suggest the reason is that so few organizations or individuals in business today understand the basics of telling the compelling story.

The Three-Act Format of Storytelling

If you believe that you aren't a storyteller, well, you probably also said in an earlier chapter that you aren't creative, didn't you? You don't have to be a natural. You just have to be interested and committed. You need to be interested not only in your own story but also in the power of a story to convey information, emotion, and understanding. You must be intrigued by how you can leverage your uniqueness into connectivity with your customers and colleagues through the presentation of your unique story. And you have to be committed to telling your story. In today's world it's not enough to create the story. You have to be committed to conveying it repeatedly to the groups and individuals who matter most to your organization. Let's face it, a story you keep to yourself has the same value as no story at all. It does you no good whatsoever to craft a story and then fail to spread it through various methods.

You must find the drama and emotion in your story, and you do that through the three-act format of storytelling. The three-act format focuses on the two critical elements of every story: the characters and the conflict they encounter. Here is the three-act format:

Act 1: Introduction of characters and conflict

Act 2: The varied attempts by the characters to resolve the conflict

Act 3: The heroic resolution of the conflict by the lead character

For example, in the classic action thriller *Die Hard*, we meet a New York detective played by Bruce Willis, as he arrives in Los Angeles to celebrate Christmas with his wife. We learn he is also there to attempt to save their estranged marriage, because he truly loves her. Meanwhile, during the office Christmas party, the wife and her coworkers are taken hostage by a group of terrorists. Notice, this is a classic act 1: the audience meets characters

Act 2

Now that you have defined the conflict, describe the pursuit of an answer to the problem. In the real world—as well as in fiction—few of us arrive at the remedy on our first attempt. Describe the varied efforts by your characters to resolve the challenges they faced and the failures they encountered along the way.

To say, "Jane was smart and got an A^+ in class," is not a great story. But to describe Jane as growing up in a poor family that had no high school graduates . . . and her need for superior grades to gain admission to college as well as her necessity for scholarships to pay for her education . . . perhaps without the support and understanding of some of her family . . . as well as her extraordinary efforts to know the material . . . makes receiving an A^+ in class a much more compelling statement.

Notice that the results she generated are identical in both presentations. However, by adding her efforts, challenges, and situations to the mix—in other words, by creating an act 2—Jane's A+ is infinitely more compelling.

To use a business model, you could say, "Tom runs a dry cleaners." Or, you could point out that Tom, faced with new competition and challenges with environmental regulations, became first a serious student and then a leading proponent of alternative cleaning methods. He courageously changed how his parents and grandparents ran the family business. Therefore, Tom creatively manages the dry cleaning establishment in a manner that serves his customers, while also becoming a public example of a "green" business.

Note that in both cases, Tom runs a drycleaner. When you relate a story that owns an act 2, you now present potential customers with a compelling reason to do business with him.

You should begin to isolate numerous aspects that detail the search for resolution that you (or your organization's founders) explored—or that your customers are currently seeking—so you can enhance the impact of your narrative. Next, write these facets you have identified in detail on your story sheet. This can effectively be a voluminous quest—as authors such as Tom Clancy and John Grisham seem to prove with every new book—or it can be as concise a pursuit as changing from your current detergent to a new one in a half-minute television commercial. My experience has always been that it is better to start with more examples than you require and then scale your story down, so you can streamline your efforts for maximum impact.

Act 3

Now, the conclusion of your story—a compelling act 3, and your opportunity to become heroic. But in order to maximize its impact, you must take steps to determine the manner in which your audience prefers your story to conclude.

I was conducting a consulting session with a team of financial advisors when this point was driven home to me through their experience. "Scott," the principal of the team told me, "we have always prided ourselves on results and returns that beat the market. And we thought we were doing a pretty good job of telling our clients and prospects that we were doing just that. However, for some reason, we were not getting our messages to have the kind of traction that delivers more of the kind of high net worth prospects any practice desires. We would constantly tell them that we were getting higher returns than the market, or than our competition, but it didn't seem to make a difference."

What would be the act 3 for *your* report? Consider several wrap-ups to your account, and write them on your story sheet. Then prepare for a vital step in the process.

Screen-Test Your Story

That financial advisor needed to discover something that the movie studios have known for decades. You have to screen-test your story, especially when you are evaluating your act 3. A CNN report from 1998 relates some big changes in major films as a result of the input of audiences at screenings prior to public release.

For example, Rupert Everett was to have a small role in Julia Roberts's film *My Best Friend's Wedding*—until the screenings clearly showed that audiences wanted much more of him in the movie. "So the ending was scrapped, the set rebuilt, and Everett's character came back for one final appearance," says the network.[7]

In the now classic movie *Fatal Attraction*, screening audiences so intensely despised Glenn Close's character that the ending was rewritten and she was killed off in a revised and much more gripping conclusion. (As we look back at them, the act 3 in each of these films is so satisfying to the audience, it is hard to imagine they could have considered any other endings.)

If the professional storytellers making multi-million-dollar films have to consider the customer to craft the best ending for their stories, you should not hesitate in seeking input on yours.

How does this process work for filmmakers? "First, test audiences are recruited from movie lines," CNN reports. "The audience sees the film for free. Afterward, each participant fills out a survey."

This survey asks for opinions similar to those you should seek from customers:

- What you thought of the story
- What five things you liked best
- What five things you liked least
- Which part of the story you liked the most
- Which characters you identified with

CNN continues, "Some members of the audience are asked to join a smaller discussion, known as a focus group. There, the process works basically the same way. 'There was a facilitator,' says Robert Kessler of a focus group he attended. 'And he basically asked people to comment on whether they liked or disliked certain characters, whether you thought certain things should have been more developed, less developed, et cetera.'"

The reason this approach is so important is best summarized by acclaimed director Ron Howard, who stated for CNN, "What I would hate to do is put the movie out there, find out that the audience is confused about something or upset about something that you could have fixed, and go, 'I had no idea they'd respond that way.'"[8]

Yet as our earlier example demonstrates, many of us in business communicate without really understanding how our audience will respond. After the financial advisor screen-tested his act 3, he reported a different reaction. "We asked a select few of our 'A' clients what was the most important result of our work for them," he told me. "Not one single client mentioned that we 'beat the market' or 'beat the competition.' It was that they got to go to the Vatican, sail on a dream cruise, or buy a second home in a vacation paradise. We realized that what we were currently promoting was a pretty important act 3 for *us*, but it wasn't the heroic resolution that *our audience* desired!" By changing the conclusion of their story to the act 3 the audience desired—and one that was also totally honest and ethical—their referrals have grown and their business has improved.

The Next Phase for the Differentiation of High Point University

Imagine now that High Point University must create a compelling story to communicate its clear and creative points of distinction. How would you do it?

Here is the answer: it would *all depend upon the audience.*

The story a parent would want to hear might be told through the character of an alumnus who developed a highly successful professional career as a result of the unique experience of being a student at High Point University. A prospective student would prefer a narrative about a young adult facing the pressures of academic performance combined with the desire for an enjoyable collegiate experience. A potential donor might wish to be enthralled by a chronicle of a corporate leader facing tremendous challenges in finding highly prepared professionals, who discovers his workforce has become more productive because of the students and graduates of HPU.

Obviously, what one finds moving will leave another cold. This should not come as a surprise. Some of the movies my wife hates are my favorites and vice versa. This, of course, is why we can pick up each day's newspaper and discover a varied selection of movies playing to various target audiences. You must customize your story to fit the audience segment you are attempting to attract.

As a Part of Distinction . . .

The old adage "build a better mousetrap and the world will beat a path to your door" is horribly incorrect and totally out of date. If the planet is unaware of your advantages—and cannot find the path to your doorway—no one will ever arrive to obtain your product.

If, however, you have developed clarity about who and what

you are and creativity that generates space between you and your competitors—and, if you have communicated those results through a compelling story that is tailored for the precise audiences you desire to attract—you have made major strides in developing the kind of distinction that all organizations and professionals covet.

Yet there is one remaining cornerstone, and it is the one that can propel you and your company to greater heights than you even imagined.

Executive Summary

I. The third of the Four Cornerstones of Distinction is Communication

    a. An organization holding a meeting put up a sign saying, "Sales cures everything!"

    b. Wrong! Sales may ease the symptoms of a current situation, or keep you on life support.

    c. Sales, perhaps, *extend* everything. It does **not** cure what ails your organization.

    d. *Distinction* is the strategy that takes an ailing organization or career and gets you on your feet and back into the race.

        i. And distinction clearly cannot be built for an organization or individual that cannot communicate.

II. A culture of "story junkies"

    a. We are a culture that loves to hear—and respond to—compelling stories.

        i. We all know the stories that are behind organizations of distinction!

            1. From Southwest's founding on a napkin, to Apple starting in a garage, we are enthralled by the stories of other organizations.

            2. The problem is that we often fail to tell our own.

        ii. "We're all just cavemen with briefcases, hungry for a wise person to tell us stories."

    b. When I returned to my small hometown to speak to the faculty of my school, my third-grade teacher's insight was powerful.

        i. She told me that while I had learned my ABCs from the disciplined rote and repetition taught by my mother and grandmother, today's students have learned their alphabet from Big Bird and Bert & Ernie of *Sesame Street*.

            1. Therefore, she concluded, they "*expect* to be entertained as they are educated."

    c. When customers know your story, and find it compelling, it can create powerful results.

    i. Apple has practically no corporate sales staff, yet some businesses reported to "Business Week" that up to 25 percent of their employees are asking to use Macs.

        1. All without a single sales call from Apple.

           a. All driven by customers who know the story.

III. The "Three-Act Format" of storytelling

  a. Inspired by Joseph Campbell's work, the "three-act" approach draws drama and emotion from your story.

    i. There are two critical elements here:

      1. Characters: the people who inhabit your story, and with whom the audience identifies

      2. Conflict: the challenges that these people encounter

  b. The three acts are:

    i. Act One: Introduction of Characters and Conflict

      1. Just like Jack Bauer of *24* being called to save the country, or Bruce Willis in *Die Hard* trying to save his wife taken captive, a powerful story places characters in a situation that creates a dilemma.

      2. It can even be as simple as a mother wanting a whiter load of laundry in a thirty-second television commercial!

      a. What conflict does your customer seek to resolve through your product or service?

      b. What challenges were facing your founders when they started your organization?

  ii. Act Two: The varied attempts by the Characters to resolve the Conflict

    1. Act Two is always the longest of the three acts.

    2. Few of us find remedy in our first attempt.

      a. Therefore, the audience also identifies with our struggle for solution.

    3. Recall all of the approaches taken by Bruce Willis' character to settle his situation.

    4. Isolate and detail the numerous aspects that your customers or founders (or you!) explored to enhance the impact of your narrative.

  iii. Act Three: The heroic resolution of the Conflict by the Characters

    1. Create a highly compelling conclusion that moves your audience to respond emotionally.

      a. You need to "screen test" your story— especially your Act Three—with test groups to ensure you are eliciting the maximum impact possible.

IV. The Power of Story in Communication at High Point University

    a. HPU discovered through this process that a story needed to be created for each of their distinctive audiences.

        i. A donor might be moved by the story of HPU alumni developing successful careers, impacting the industry she cared most about.

        ii. Prospective students would be more compelled to attend via a story about young adults facing the pressures of academic performance—combined with the desire for an enjoyable collegiate experience.

    b. The lesson here is that *every* organization and *each* professional must craft multiple stories that are targeted to specific audiences.

V. "Build a better mousetrap" isn't true anymore!

    a. The cliché is horrible, incorrect, and totally out of date!

    b. If the world is unaware of your product—and doesn't know how to get to your door—no one will ever arrive to obtain what you are making!

    c. If, however, you have taken your clarity and creativity—and communicated those differentiated aspects through a compelling story—you have made major strides in creating distinction.

Action Steps, Questions, and Ideas

- Begin your story sheet. Ask yourself, What conflict did I desire to resolve when I began my business career? Or what challenge did the founders of the company seek to overcome when they started their business?

- On your story sheet, list several of the various attempts that either you or your organization's leaders tried to solve the conflict you initially indicated.

- What is the heroic resolution of your conflict?

- Write four specific ways you will screen-test your story.

- How have you varied your story to meet the unique needs of your different audiences?

Eight

The Fourth Cornerstone: Customer-Experience Focus

Comedian Jeff Foxworthy was joking about the phrases that we all utter without thinking. I laughed out loud when he mentioned that people hunting for a lost item often absent-mindedly announce, "I found it in the last place I looked!" Well, of course you did! Once you came across it, why would you continue searching?

I feel that way when I'm asked about whether an organization should have a "customer-experience" focus. I'm always thinking, "Well, where *else* could you focus? And, why would you keep on searching?"

Think about it for a moment: is it productive to focus internally, on the politics and structure of an organization? Obviously those areas require consideration, examination, and care. But if that's your *primary* area of concentration, it seems to me that your attention is in the wrong place. The same is true if your focal point is on the market and your share price. We know from a historical perspective that organizations that are differentiated from their competition and distinct in the marketplace are the winners over the long haul; yet the market often tends to reward incremental, short-term gains when viewed through the lens of daily trading.

The purpose of this chapter is to demonstrate why the focus of you and your organization should be squarely on the experience you are creating for your customers. It will also illustrate the fundamental difference between "customer service" and the "customer experience"—and present the five specific steps you must take to create the "Ultimate Customer Experience."™ In addition, the chapter will explain why those organizations claiming to have a "value added" program are probably not providing their customers with nearly enough value.

What's It All About?

Early in my career, I was asked to provide my definition of "business." Over the years, we have all heard the standards: "the purpose of business is to make a profit" or "the purpose of business is to obtain and retain customers profitably." Legendary management guru Peter Drucker said, "There is only one valid definition of business purpose: to create a customer."

My meager attempt was this: the purpose of any business is to profitably create experiences so compelling to the customers that their loyalty becomes assured. Yet, if you drill deep into the definition, you'll discover that it means that a "customer-experience focus" is primary. Your ability to profitably deliver upon that effort will determine both the success and the distinction of your organization—and you.

The Definition of *Customer Focus*

When your efforts—and your organization's actions—are wrapped up in "creating experiences so compelling that loyalty is assured," you have reached the point that this cornerstone advocates. It is the echelon where the customer's experience is at the center of every decision the organization makes—at all levels. Distinct organizations integrate this focus thoroughly into every action they take.

This characterization gets to the heart of the difference between the culture of "it's who we are" as opposed to the approach of "it's a part of the things we have to do." Customers realize that "what you do" can easily change with economic fads or organizational whims. They know that "who you are" is a basic expression of what you stand for—and what you will *continue* to be. It is the embodiment of the old adage that "actions speak louder than words."

It means that centering our focus on the customer is a decision we have made about how we are going to exist, now and forever. It's not just a short-term method we are executing because our competition is too. (Which is exactly the approach that many organizations take, and was described earlier as one of the Three Destroyers of Differentiation.)

The blog, Customers Are Always, offers its definition of a customer-focused strategy as "a plan that emphasizes the needs of a particular customer segment over that of the organization."[1] And, Maria Palma posted a nice addition to this concept on the blog when she wrote, "A strategy is not 'customer-focused' when a company is obsessed with the numbers and has the scarcity mentality. Instead of asking themselves, 'Is this for the greater good of our customers?', they're constantly asking, 'Did we make our sales goals?'"[2]

To create a compelling differentiation in today's market, it's not enough for organizations and professionals of distinction to implement a "customer-focused" strategy. Remember, our cornerstone states: distinction is created by developing a customer-*experience* focus. In other words, concentrating on customers is not enough if you want to become a true market leader. You must take it to an even higher level and focus on the creation of *experiences* for your clients and prospects.

Aren't Service and Experience the Same?

My work exposes me to many individuals and organizations that have yet to explore the fundamental difference between providing "customer service" and creating a "customer experience." This is because there are three separate and distinct levels of customer interaction. For an organization to excel, it must examine *each* of these levels as unique and create a plan to strategically improve performance at every level.

Level One: Processing—the basic elements of the transaction; the aspects that the customer has a right to expect you to deliver upon because they have chosen to spend money with you and your organization.

Level Two: Service—the steps you and your organization will undertake to make processing more efficient, palatable, enjoyable, or friendly to your customers to enhance the likelihood they will repeat their business.

Level Three: Experience—the commitment—as well as the actual execution of specific strategies—to create the element of emotion. This results in an intensely personal connection for customers. It is only at this point that loyalty from the client toward your organization (or you) is generated.

The attainment of these levels is progressive. If you fail in terms of processing—for example, if the food at the restaurant isn't properly prepared or I had to wait an extended period after the time for which I had reserved my table—then the higher levels of interaction have little traction. If my flight is three hours late arriving at O'Hare, I really don't care how hot the coffee was that the flight attendants served. However, when the flight's on time and uneventful, then receiving a nice cup of java enhances my evaluation of your organization's ability to provide me with what I want.

This morning, after taking our sons to school, I went into our local coffee shop, Higher Grounds, to pick up my wife Tammy's favorite morning beverage. I think it's a pretty complicated concoction. She wants an iced mocha, skim milk, with an extra shot of espresso, and just a light touch of whipped cream on top.

This morning's drink was prepared perfectly. (Level One: Processing.) The line in the coffee shop moved quickly, and the place is a clean and inviting environment. (Level Two: Service.) When I approached the counter, I was greeted with, "Good morning, Mr. McKain! How's the book coming along?" (Well, you can imagine that when you are working hard to complete a manuscript, it's a pretty emotional thing to have someone concerned!) And at the point where the barista behind the machine asked, "Picking up a 'Tammy'?" I had absolutely reached the point of Experience. All I had to do was ask for a "Tammy," and the barista knew the formula for her favorite drink. That's not just a customer focus—that is a customer-*experience* focus. As I'm writing this, I only now realized that I don't know if the iced mochas are more or less expensive at Higher Grounds than at Starbucks. It's irrelevant.

Creating a Customer Experience Focus from the Top

If you are in a position of significant leadership at your organization, the creation of the customer-experience focus begins with your vision. Are you willing to seek what is now commonly called the "voice of the customer"? Do you have feedback systems in place that will provide you with unaltered evaluations from your clients? And perhaps most important, are you willing to ask at every juncture how each action of your company will impact customers and create more compelling differentiation for your organization?

Currently, I'm dealing with an organization that has had a transition in leadership. The new CEO is completely committed to changing the culture of the organization and putting his stake in the ground that his leadership legacy will be one of a concerted and disciplined focus on the client experience. The challenge is, many of his managers believe this is a "nice" approach, but want to delegate this effort to a single client-services department. One manager even intimated to me that he wanted the "client people to take care of the customers so I can just do my job."

The new CEO faces the uphill battle of convincing this manager that his opinion about the business is totally wrong. If the manager believes that customers in today's marketplace are somebody else's job, then *he* should be out of a job! If you are unsuccessful in creating distinction in the marketplace through the four cornerstones—and particularly this one—then it becomes ensured that a mediocre voyage on the sea of sameness is the best you'll achieve. And, please understand that failure is a definite possibility.

I admire the new CEO, but my esteem is slight compared to the manner in which his colleagues will respect and appreciate him in a few years. He not only has an occasion to lead an organization; he is taking advantage of an opportunity to pioneer a new level of client connectivity and distinction. If you are the leader of a company—regardless of the size—do you have similar courage and commitment?

Creating a Customer Experience Focus from Elsewhere

But what if you're not the person in charge? How can you create this point of distinction for yourself?

My answer is not an easy one. However, in all honesty, it is the only one available. You just have to do it. You must examine your specific area of corporate responsibility and become the CEO of your "customer-experience focused" mini-firm within your organization.

If your management imitates an ostrich and puts its organizational head in the sand during these times of economic volatility, you have to take the initiative and responsibility to do all you can do for your customers—and yourself—by personally employing these customer-focused distinction strategies. If you are successful in this effort, you may find that one (or more) of these five circumstances occurs:

1. Your success moves you to a higher level of responsibility within your organization.

2. Your distinction attracts the attention of a competitor with the proper vision and strategy.

3. You outlast the current management team, and your achievements and client connectivity make you highly desirable to a new regime.

4. One of your customers realizes that you would be an enormous asset on his or her team and offers you a position with that organization.

5. You discover that you would like to be the captain of your own ship and become an entrepreneur.

Yet, as corny as it sounds, these should be residual reasons for creating a compelling experience for your clients or customers. The fundamental reason is that it is *purely the right thing to do!* It is executing for your customers the very connection that you desire when *you* are the client. It is becoming the living embodiment of the golden rule that we have likely been encouraged to live by, regardless of the specific cultural or religious tradition in which we were raised.

Cultures everywhere acknowledge the wisdom of this rule. Hindus learn in Mahabharata 5:1517, "This is the sum of duty: do not do to others what would cause pain if done to you." Islam teaches in Number 13 of Imam Al-Nawawi's Forty Hadiths: "None of you [truly] believes until he wishes for his brother what he wishes for himself." Followers of Confucianism learn in Analects 15:23, "Do not do to others what you do not want them to do to you."[3] As a Christian, I believe the words of the Holy Bible in Luke 6:31, "As ye would that men should do to you, do ye also to them likewise."

My friend and colleague, Dr. Tony Alessandra lectures on "The Platinum Rule," which is "Do unto others the way they want to be done unto." Regardless of your individual beliefs, it is almost impossible to imagine a detrimental outcome from executing strategies that place customers at the center of every action that you and your organization take.

Creating the Ultimate Customer Experience

To attain this focus, you need to create what I have been (for more than two decades) calling the "Ultimate Customer Experience" (UCE). You can find a detailed examination of UCE in my previous book, *ALL Business Is Show Business*. However, for our purposes, here's a brief look at how you can produce and implement a UCE.

Step One: Ask a Question

The first step to create the UCE is to take a legal pad and (individually or with your team) ask the question, "What would happen if *everything* went exactly right?" —then record all of the responses.

Doing this is more complex than it might first appear. If everything went exactly right, how many times would the phone ring before it was answered? What percentage of your calls should be fielded by a live person instead of via technology? What sensations would be experienced by customers when they walk into your store? The single most important factor here is to keep drilling down to the smallest aspects of your interactions with customers and prospects and constantly pushing for what would have to happen for that contact to be exactly right.

I've heard that Starbucks does not allow its associates to wear cologne or perfume on the days they work. The reason is obvious. When you walk in the coffee shop, Starbucks wants you to savor the aroma of the coffee, not wonder if you are inhaling Chanel No. 5 or Calvin Klein's Obsession. You must examine your interaction with your customers and prospects with extraordinary precision in order to get it exactly right. That's the standard of the Ultimate Customer Experience.

Step Two: Engage Your Customer in the Process

When there is enhanced interaction, what follows is enhanced connectivity. Therefore, it is imperative that you involve your clients in the process of creating the UCE. After all, how can it be ultimate if it fails to deliver what the customer *really* wants?

The most basic—and often most powerful—approach to involving the customer is simply to ask, "If you could describe the ultimate experience of doing business with an organization like ours, what would that be?" (Then you *listen!*)

The fundamental challenge that so many organizations and professionals experience with this approach is that it is *counterintuitive*. When a customer presents you with an answer that provides an opportunity to initiate a transaction, you may find it hard to resist the chance to "close the sale." As your client answers your UCE question, she may state that she seeks something that you already provide. Your natural inclination may be to butt in and say, "We can do that!"

At this juncture, from the customer's perspective, this entire process appears to be nothing more than a sophisticated sales call—not an attempt to improve the customer's experience. The situation might also mean that you unintentionally inhibit a relationship. Just as in your personal situations with friends and family, customers desire to be listened to and appreciated. When you attempt to push the customer and close a transaction, you may miss out on hearing highly insightful and revealing information.

Step Three: Sync the Information

Next, match the steps you internally developed to create the UCE to the hopes and dreams that have been expressed through this process by your customers.

In some areas, the two may fit together quite nicely—in other words, what the customers told you they wanted in the UCE and what you outlined are highly similar. However, I have also found some outcomes to be highly conflicting. If this is the case, realize that you are creating the UCE to engage your customers! You must give them the benefit of the doubt.

On the other hand, temper this aspect with a point we've previously discussed: sometimes your vision of the future is more enhanced and profound than your customers'. *Your* insight is required to build the UCE as well.

Step Four: Outline the Roadblocks

Another question is vital to the development of the UCE: "What roadblocks prevent us from executing the UCE for every customer or prospect at every point of interaction?" Make a list of the barriers and analyze them. Some will be outdated corporate policies, while others will be misguided strategies. All of these UCE obstructions should be intensely scrutinized and, hopefully, eliminated.

Step Five: Execute!

If only it were that simple, right?

Look, as the vice chairman of an organization that owns nineteen affiliates, I know that none of us—no matter our position within the company, from owner to custodian—can snap our fingers and put any strategy into action.

So many times, the UCE boils down to a commitment by employees throughout an organization. A couple of days ago, a United Airlines employee stood behind the ticket kiosk with my driver's license in one hand, my boarding pass in the other, and a computer screen with my reservation in front of her. She was literally surrounded with forms that had my name on them, yet she never used "Scott" or "McKain" at any point in our interaction. It's impossible to create an experience—much less the UCE—without executing those little points of contact properly. The CEO can insist upon it—yet, if not actually delivered by a frontline employee, the customer often fails to feel as if his experience has a customer focus.

However, please consider this: Why do you suppose that we constantly read and hear about the same companies all the time? You know the ones: Starbucks, Apple, Southwest, Nordstrom. I believe the reason is because so unbelievably few organizations actually execute on the promise of the Ultimate Customer Experience. That's how breathtakingly difficult it *really* is! However, the spectacular success of these organizations should also clearly display how critical it is to endeavor to achieve a UCE.

Barack Obama's Focus on the "Customer"

Much has been made by the political pundits on the connection that Barack Obama established with his supporters throughout the process we have been discussing. Let me give you an individual perspective--because, at the end of the day, the customer experience is intensely personal.

First, however, this disclaimer: I did not contribute financially to either of the presidential candidates. My vote and support is a private matter. However, I did sign up online so that I could receive the messages sent to supporters on both major candidate's Web sites. Throughout the campaign, Obama's team was in much more frequent and personal contact with their list. Nothing, though, is a better example than the email I received on election night.

While sitting at home and watching CNN on that historic evening, I saw a report stating that President-elect Obama would be heading to Grant Park to speak to the massive throng of supporters gathered to cheer their successful leader. Just then, I heard the tone from my iPhone that I'd just received a new mail message. I was astonished to read the following:

Friend—

I'm about to head to Grant Park to talk to everyone gathered there, but I wanted to write to you first.

We just made history.

And I don't want you to forget how we did it.

You made history every single day during this campaign— every day you knocked on doors, made a donation, or talked to your family, friends, and neighbors about why you believe it's time for change.

I want to thank all of you who gave your time, talent, and passion to this campaign.

We have a lot of work to do to get our country back on track, and I'll be in touch soon about what comes next.

But I want to be very clear about one thing . . .

All of this happened because of you.

> Thank you,
> Barack

Well, in all honesty, I didn't knock on any doors, or make a donation, or give any time or talent to the campaign. However, the simple fact that *someone*—whether Obama himself, or the extraordinarily customer experienced-focused people he has chosen for his team—first had the insight to think of this, and then execute it at precisely the right moment, is extraordinarily impressive. It is an epitome of the Ultimate Customer Experience.

Re-examine the message and notice its perfection in creating an Ultimate Customer Experience. The new president is getting ready to go speak to several hundred thousand people . . . but *first*, he wanted to send *me* this email! (Okay, I realize that millions undoubtedly received this identical message, too. However, that's not what you are thinking as you're sitting there reading it. It created a personal effect, and connection.) And, he told me that all of this happened because of me! Finally, the 44th president of the United States signed my message simply, "Barack."

Yet, when I examine the emails and other messages I receive from companies where I actually *do* spend money, I often find them oddly impersonal and formal. There is little to no recognition of my importance to the company, even though, as a customer, I—and those like me—are their lifeblood. Organizations seem to focus on the mailing list more than what the message to that list conveys. They seem to center upon the communication strategy infinitely more than the communication quality.

The electronic message I received that night from the Obama campaign is a perfect example of how an Ultimate Customer Experience blends both technology and strategy with the intense personalization and heightened emotional connection that customers covet.

The "Value-Added" Approach

We have all observed many organizations that—rather than execute a customer-experience focused approach and deliver UCEs—instead offer "value-added" inducements to their clients and prospects.

Here's my fundamental problem with this strategy: when we do not possess enough of something that we want or need, we desire to *add* to what we have until we reach a point of satisfaction. In other words, if the tea isn't sweet enough for us, we add sugar or a substitute until it reaches the taste we crave. If we don't have enough savings to provide for our retirement, we make deposits into our account until we reach a satisfactory balance. Note the fundamental reason that we feel required to augment and increase what we have is that we didn't possess some vital element in the quantity that we desired.

So, here are two questions for you:

1. When an organization approaches you with a "value-added" proposition, does that mean that the company failed to provide you with enough value in what it had *originally* offered—so now it feels required to bolt on some more?

2. When a professional discusses her "value add" with a prospect, is this approach merely an attempt to recover from an inability to deliver what the customer really wanted in the first place?

If you are truly connected to customers, then providing significant and distinct value through your products and services—and assisting clients in growing their own results—should be an integral part of every action. It's not something that has to be added as a separate function.

When you are required to add something to an existing mix, then (by definition) it means that element is not a part of the original article—or is available in a quantity so limited that the client has become disconnected. Visionary leaders and insightful organizations focus their attention on their customers in a manner that creates growth and strategic differentiation for their clients. Through that effort, they cannot help gaining both for themselves as well.

Do You Really Believe . . .

- Do you think that Nordstrom has workshops to teach associates its value-*added* proposition? I don't! I believe that the customer experience has been woven into the fabric of everything the company does.

- Do you believe that Steve Jobs gathered the troops before the introduction of the iPhone and asked, "Okay, great product. Now, what's our value *add*?"

- Did Howard Schultz remind his baristas to "remember the customer's name" when he closed every Starbucks for training because it is a good idea to create *added* value? Of course not.

All of the elements that create true value for the customer are viewed by these organizations as *intrinsic!* They describe the very essence of what the organization is all about. This means that what distinct organizations deliver cannot be segmented into what is "value added" and what is not.

If you say you are a sales organization with a value-added program, your clients will perceive you for exactly what you are—a bunch of sales guys and gals with a product to hawk and a bag of goodies that you'll sprinkle their way if they buy from you. In other words, you are exactly like everyone else who is calling on them.

My belief is that organizations and individuals need to look higher than a value-added program. We all need to reach for *strategic differentiation.*

In other words, the strategies we are executing as an organization are so focused—and provide so much value to the customers from their very conception—that we never find ourselves having to develop and implement a separate program to add value. Our differentiation is not an add-on or option because true distinction is always essential to who we are.

My experience, however, has been that many organizations view the customer as just *one* of the facets they must deal with to build a successful business, instead of their very reason for existence. Numerous professionals may give lip service to customers as the chief priority. However, when you examine how they spend their time, they value other aspects as infinitely more essential.

I have a considerable disagreement with a sales executive

(whom I tremendously respect on a personal level) at a company where I have done a significant amount of work. He states, "We are primarily a sales organization. Our 'value add' enhances our access to customers and prospects and elevates our visibility in the marketplace. However, if someone on our team is hitting his or her numbers without using our value-add program, then it's an optional resource for that person."

Here's the reason for my resistance to this line of thinking: Do you think Nordstrom managers would ever—in a million years—say to the sales team, "Look, if you are hitting your numbers in women's shoe sales, you can sell them any way you want"? There is *zero* chance they would ever take that approach! Nordstrom would teach that its way of creating the experience and dealing with customers is just "how it's done." It is certainly not optional in any manner whatsoever.

Les Schwab Tires would never, ever suggest, "You know, if your store is moving enough tires to make your goals, just walk to the cars. In fact, why not let customers come up to the counter just like our competitors do? Running is optional if your store is hitting its numbers."

High Point University would never be the same if President Qubein announced at a faculty and staff meeting, "Admissions and endowment goals have been exceeded, so don't worry about that 'fun environment' stuff anymore. Just do your jobs." In fact, Qubein would be the first to dramatically emphasize to his team that creating the fun environment is their job—it is *just the way things are done* at HPU. In fact, it is chiefly because of the execution of the customer-experience focus that High Point University was hailed by *U.S. News and World Report* as number one of the "up and coming" colleges in the nation!

It All Comes Together . . .

Notice how all of the Cornerstones of Distinction are coming together?

The company that will not develop clarity will find it enormously difficult to execute a strategy of customer-experience focus. If you haven't defined who and what you really are, it becomes impossible to deliver experiences to customers that are congruent with your organization's focus. (Obviously, because you don't *have* a focus!) If you failed to be creative, and are therefore unsuccessful at communicating any points of distinction you've created, then the expectations of the prospect or customer aren't in alignment with a customer-experience focus.

> Center your efforts on strategic differentiation through a customer experience focus.

However, let's reverse the outlook to one that is positive. If you are clear about what you stand for, you can develop the precision necessary to deliver to admiring customers the compelling experiences that ensure loyalty. You can communicate your individual and organizational distinction, in part because you're focused on customers—and because your actions are aligned. You truly "practice what you preach." The customer-experience focus is the right place for you to concentrate your efforts. It is the final piece in the puzzle to build distinction as you differentiate yourself from your competition.

There You Have It

The Four Cornerstones of Distinction are now in place, and you can begin to build an organization that is differentiated and a career that is a hallmark of excellence.

Our final chapter will wrap a ribbon around our package, as we build upon our cornerstones.

Executive Summary

I. The third of the Four Cornerstones of Distinction is Customer Experience Focus

    a. If you are seeking distinction, where *else* would you look?

    b. Yet, many organizations focus internally, on the politics and structure of their company.

        i. Obviously, that's an important issue; however, if it is your primary area of concentration, your attention is in the wrong place.

II. The definition of business

   a. My definition of what a "business" is all about is: "The purpose of any business is to profitably create experiences so compelling to its customers that their loyalty becomes assured."

   b. If you drill into that definition, you'll discover that it means that inherent in the process of business is found a "customer experience focus."

      i. Your ability to deliver upon this effort will determine the success of your organization or your career.

III. Customer experience focus is who we are!

   a. Distinctive organizations view a focus upon the customer experience as an integral part of who they are.

      i. Non-differentiated companies and professionals view it as "one of the things we have to do."

      ii. That difference is subtle, yet profound.

   b. A customer experience focus "emphasizes the needs of customers over that of the organization."

      i. It's not customer experienced focused when you are obsessed with numbers and have a scarcity mentality.

IV. "Customer service" and the "customer experience" are NOT the same!

a. There are three levels at which you interact with your customers: *Processing, Service*, and *Experience*.

b. Success in delivering at one level means the customer allows you the opportunity to advance higher on the scale.

c. The higher the level of interaction, the more engaged the customer.

   i. Engaged customers become loyal customers!

d. Level One: Processing

   i. Processing consists of the basic elements of the transaction.

   ii. Processing contains what the customer has a right to expect because they have chosen to do business with you.

e. Level Two: Service

   i. Service consists of the steps you take to ensure Processing is efficient, palatable, and enjoyable for the customer.

   ii. Points such as "being friendly," and "answering the phone promptly" would fall under Service.

f. Level Three: Experience

   i. The customer experience adds the elements of *personalization* and *emotion*.

ii. When you creatively execute strategies that cause the customer to feel you are offering a solution that is intensely personal to their needs—and when they are emotionally connected to you and your organization—you have created a customer experience.

iii. The customer experience transcends transactions.

iv. The customer experience is where customer loyalty is created.

V. Creating the customer experience focus

a. From the top:

i. CEO's and top managers seeking to create the customer experience focus should:

1. Specifically communicate your vision of the experience.

2. Listen to the "voice of the customer."

3. Have a feedback system in place that will provide you with unaltered evaluations from your clients.

4. Ask at every juncture how each action of your company will impact customers and create more compelling experiences.

b. From elsewhere in the business:

    i. If you do not have top leadership with the same vision regarding the customer experience focus, you need to:

      1. Examine your area of personal responsibility and become the CEO of your own "mini-firm" that does have the proper focus within your organization.

      2. Take the initiative and the responsibility to do all you can for your customers.

        a. This approach is simply the "right thing to do."

        b. And, it will have residual benefit for you and your career that can be substantial and long-lasting.

VI. Steps to creating the "Ultimate Customer Experience"™

  a. Step One: Ask a question

    i. Ask yourself or your team, "What would happen if *everything* went *exactly* right?"

      1. Record the responses

      2. A more complex exercise than it first appears

      3. Be highly detailed and precise about your answers

  b. Step Two: Engage your customer in the process

   i. Now, ask your customers, "If you could describe the ultimate experience of doing business with an organization like ours, what would that be?"

     1. Record their responses

     2. Listen!

       a. During their descriptions, customers will often point out something that you or your organization is already doing.

       b. This is *not* a time to be selling or telling! If you start talking about your strong points, the customer now perceives they have been deceived, that this is not a process to serve them better, but instead to sell them more.

  ii. Step Three: Sync the information

     1. Match the steps you internally developed to the points your customers have identified.

     2. Where these points sync are high priority items.

 iii. Step Four: Outline the roadblocks

     1. Identify the specific areas where executing these steps will be most difficult for you and your organization.

       a. Some will be outdated policies, others misguided strategies.

        b. Hopefully, all roadblocks will be eliminated.

    iv. Step Five: Execute!

        1. Easy to say, infinitely harder to do!

        2. Delivering the UCE depends upon the personal dedication and discipline of every person within the organization.

VII. "Value added" *isn't* "customer experience focused!"

  a. When an organization says it has a "value added" approach or inducement, what does it REALLY mean?

  b. When we are required to supplement or augment something, it usually means we didn't possess enough of a vital element (in the quantity that we desired) in the first place.

    i. For example, if the tea isn't sweet enough, we ADD sugar.

    ii. If the taste is great we do not feel the need to add *anything*!

  c. Therefore, distinct organizations are so connected to customers that they provide significant value as an integral part of every action.

  d. Value does not have to be "added" when it is a part of the very fabric of your business!

      i. Nordstrom doesn't "add value" to the way they sell shoes. It's just the way they do it.

     ii. Apple didn't "add value" to the iPhone. It's just the way they designed and built it.

   iii. Starbucks doesn't "add value" via baristas being friendly and remembering your name. It's just who they are.

   iv. High Point University doesn't "add value" to the student experience. It's a direct result of the values they personify.

e. When you have strategic differentiation, you are so focused—and provide so much value—there is no need for a separate program, or add-on option.

      i. True distinction is always congruent to who you are.

VIII. It all comes together.

a. Without Clarity, how can you have a focus on the Customer Experience?

b. Without Creativity, how can you deliver compelling Communication?

      i. When you are clear about what you stand for, you can develop the precision necessary to deliver to admiring customers the compelling experiences that ensure loyalty.

ii. You can communicate your individual and organizational distinction because you are focused on your customers.

c. With this, the Four Cornerstones of Distinction are in place—the foundation of an organization (or a professional). This is a hallmark of excellence.

Action Steps, Questions, and Ideas

- What would happen if everything went exactly right in terms of the customer experience? Be highly specific in your answers.

- Write down how you have specifically involved your customers in helping you develop your strategies to enhance relationships. If you haven't already done so, then list the ways that you will get them engaged.

- What are the roadblocks preventing the UCE?

Nine
Different Is Better

Long after Kern's Grill closed its doors in Crothersville, Indiana, Ted's Restaurant continued to thrive. Its owner, Ted Zollman, was very clear about what his place of business was—and wasn't. Unlike Alvie Kern, Ted attempted to replicate neither the speed of McDonald's transactions nor the menu of Burger King. He got creative with his promotions and with his service. He communicated in a personal and charismatic manner with all who entered his establishment, and he created a UCE for just about everyone who dined there. Later, after his passing, Ted's family sold the restaurant, and it remains in business to this day. Ted Zollman ran a small business—but, for me, he looms large among professionals skilled in providing Ultimate Customer Experiences.

Inspiring Figures of Distinction

I stand in awe of the accomplishments of Dr. Nido Qubein at High Point University. Although it has always been a wonderful institution, it has only recently begun to receive national attention and distinction. In my opinion, this is because of the remarkable job that Dr. Qubein has done to differentiate the school from its myriad of worthy competitors. A trip to the campus is one of the most invigorating and inspiring visits anyone could have. You can almost feel the electricity in the air, and it is contagious.

As we have discussed, HPU has clarity about its purpose and has developed remarkably creative approaches to campus life and academics that are reverberating across the nation and—guided by its eloquent president—are being communicated to its varied audiences of students, parents, prospects, faculty, staff, and donors in an extraordinary manner. Does HPU provide an Ultimate Student Experience? The proof is in the results. Applications for admissions are going through the roof, and to meet this demand, the school is investing $225 million in new buildings, academic programs, athletics, student life, technology, and campus improvements that will bring to the university more than eight hundred thousand square feet of new construction.

Nido Qubein also clearly demonstrates his personal commitment to these principles. He teaches a class that is required for all freshmen: Real World 101: The President's Seminar on Life Skills. Not only does this class prepare HPU students for what life will bring them, both as college students and as graduates—it also means that *every* student will have spent time communicating with and getting to know the president of the university.

I deeply admire my best friend, Tim Durham, founder and chairman of Obsidian Enterprises. As you may have read in one of my previous books, Tim was crystal clear about what we were—and weren't—going to invest in as we built our company. Under Tim's leadership we were creative, both in management techniques and in financial structure, so we could rapidly grow. We communicated our vision to all of our acquisitions and the customers of those companies. And we are constantly striving, with Tim's support, to create distinction in the marketplace—an example of which, Pyramid Coach, was discussed in this book.

My work with Old Mutual has been another reminder that global giants can create UCEs for individual clients when the organization's leaders are firmly committed to building a company of distinction. My longtime friend and colleague Bruce Johnston, CEO of Old Mutual Investment Partners (OMIP), first involved me with the company. He has been a visionary leader in moving his teams toward strategic differentiation. Through Johnston's efforts—and the engagement and support of the CEO of Old Mutual Capital, Julian Sluyters—OMIP now provides comprehensive education and consulting for financial advisors on strategies to grow their practices in a manner unique to their industry. The result has been that by differentiating themselves in this manner in the crowded mutual fund marketplace, Old Mutual has done a remarkable job of weathering the current storm in the financial markets. OMIP has taken market share away from competitors that currently possess better-known brands, but are displaying themselves to their clients to be organizations of lesser distinction.

Johnston's counterpart on the insurance side of the business, John Phelps, has also created a program of differentiation. Taking the "Old Mutual Road Show" to thirty-one cities in eleven weeks to personally meet with Old Mutual's independent agents is a fundamental part of Phelps's strategy. His goal is to provide cutting-edge information and unique tools to assist insurance professionals in their efforts to more competently and compassionately discover and support the needs of their clients and prospects.

Guess what? When you create compelling experiences for your clients, they do the same for their customers—and, they remember your product in a more frequent and more sizable manner.

My Best Teacher

Of all the businesspeople I have known, however, I learned the most about business and customers from my late father, Dallas McKain.

As I mentioned earlier, my mom and dad owned the solitary grocery store in our rural community. After Dad worked for several years as a truck driver, meat cutter, then assistant grocery store manager, my parents finally rounded up the financing necessary to purchase a store of their own in our hometown. Like the financial situation of many entrepreneurial couples, the financial future of our entire family depended upon the success of that little store, and both worked there tirelessly.

I remember Mom and Dad being somewhat shocked and highly concerned over the closing of Kern's Grill just across the street. For a family business to go under so quickly because of what my folks perceived to be issues totally out of their control caused them enormous consternation. Then we received what was, for us, extremely tragic news: a new supermarket was going to be built on the other end of our town.

It was going to have at least twice our shelf space. It would have a shiny linoleum floor, compared to our old wooden one. It would have multiple checkout lanes, while we had a solitary, outdated NCR cash register. It would have what one good ol' boy called "the seeing-eye door." You would just walk up and it would open! (How could it know?) We certainly didn't have anything like that.

Many in our small town predicted that McKain's Market would be the next casualty to larger and supposedly more sophisticated competition. However, Dad was just not ready to throw in the towel.

I reminisce now in what an old-timer back home calls "slack-jawed amazement" at some of my father's decisions. He was armed with only a high school education and instinct. He had no management training and had never previously owned a business, yet he made remarkable choices in the face of a sea change the size of "the perfect storm" for his little store. He reduced the number of employees to only those who could—and would—remember every customer's name and make customers feel as if they were at home. He *cut* the number of hours our store was going to be open, instead of what most do—stay open later to match the national competitor.

Dad's belief was that tired, stressed-out, worn-out employees do not create happy customers. Only about 5 percent of purchases were made during 20 percent of the time we were open—so, he reasoned, chop off some of those hours and rest your staff while reducing your overhead.

He emphasized the areas of service where he could differentiate our store from what he knew instinctively that the new competition would do. He planted himself behind the counter and hand-cut and hand-wrapped almost every piece of meat the store sold. He designed a truck he could take to farms, so he could custom-butcher cattle. His thinking was that not only would it provide a significant new source of revenue for the store, but it would also be considerably more difficult for the farmer's family to then buy bread and milk at the competition when "good ol' Dallas" had literally been on their farm helping them.

He also concentrated on what we were not and could never become: a low-price leader. He knew that we would, by no means, be able to sell Green Giant creamed corn, for example, less expensively than a national competitor. Therefore, we would have to be *different* because we certainly could not be cheaper.

I still clearly remember the day the competition opened. A nearby radio station did a live remote broadcast there—quite an event for our little town. It was Saturday, the busiest day in the grocery business, and as we drove by, we saw their parking lot was already jam-packed.

We entered McKain's Market practically in the shadow of the now-closed Kern's Grill and turned on the lights. It was seven a.m.

My sister, Shelley, made herself busy by pulling shelves. (That means you reach back into the shelves and pull the older cans to the front so that stock sells before the newer product. If you just put the newest delivery at the front, the product in the back never changes.) Mom shuffled papers in the tiny store office, and Dad was behind the meat counter grinding beef into hamburger for that day's sales. I took my spot behind our sole cash register, waiting to check out customers.

Imagine our feeling of depression and desperation when we had yet to serve our first customer *four hours* later! By that point, Mom was crying, and Dad was talking to himself. Shelley pulled every can in the store, and I plopped myself onto a stool to read the latest edition of *Superman*.

But as the clock was striking eleven, the door to our little store opened and in walked the least likely customer imaginable. For the purposes of my story, let's call him Leland—and he was what everyone in our town would call "quite a character." Suffice it to say, his reputation was less than sterling and his demeanor less than elegant.

Leland wrestled a shopping cart out of the stack and pulled out a slip of paper that, because of its neatness and precision, was obviously written by his wife. He started down the first aisle, muttering to himself and roughly throwing the items from his list into his cart.

As he continued to shop, my curiosity got the best of me, and by the time he arrived to be checked out, I was bursting to ask the question I had been pondering. I just could not keep it inside. It was a defining moment in my life—the point I realized I was endlessly fascinated with the behavior of customers and the differentiation of organizations.

"Leland," I began softly—after all, he was an adult and I was a mere high school kid—"*you* are our first customer today."

He arched his right eyebrow and grunted.

"What I have to know is this, and I hope you don't mind me asking," I quickly added. "Why are you here? All of our so-called friends have left us today and gone to the supermarket owned by big shots from elsewhere. Why did you decide to come *here* instead of shop *there*?" I will never forget what happened next.

Leland's face turned red as the beets in his basket. He pawed his left boot awkwardly across our wooden floor. He glanced up at me and gruffly said, "Aw, come on. You know why."

I was at a loss. I just didn't get it. I had no idea why he had selected McKain's Market on that monumental moment. "No, Leland. I'm sorry. I don't know why."

Summoning up all of his communication ability, Leland looked me in the eye, a wry smile evolving from the right corner of his lips, and proudly announced, "'Cause you guys *like me!*"

I'm a bit ashamed to admit that what popped into my head were words I would never utter: *No, we don't!*

Of course, my next thought was, *But we sure do* now!

Leland continued to shop with us, despite the advantages of our competition. Eventually, almost everyone else in town came back too. Dad's little joke was that even if you only bought a pack of gum, we were going to carry it out to your car for you unless you wrestled us to the ground.

The marketplace in a small town in Indiana voted with their hard-earned grocery money and their feet. They decided that paying just a little more to shop where you received an Ultimate Customer Experience was a great investment.

One time when I called home from college, I noticed Dad seemed a little bit down and not himself. When I asked why, he gave me the news: the supermarket had announced it was going to close and leave town.

"Good grief, Dad," I exclaimed, "you won! You beat the big store!"

"Aw, son," he replied, "what about those folks who work there? I just can't hire them all, and I don't want them to be out of work."

Of course, his sincere response was a perfect reflection of why people in Crothersville, Indiana, had considered the alternatives—and chosen to do business with *him*.

And that is how a simple meat cutter from a small Hoosier town inspired a business philosophy that his grateful son now has the privilege to write and teach to major corporations and visionary professionals around the world.

You Can Do It

The easiest tactic for you is to merely continue what you are currently doing. You may perceive that to "not make waves" and to "keep on keeping on" are the safest things for you to do. Let me emphatically state my belief that in the vast majority of cases, this is the most *dangerous* approach.

Because of the Three Destroyers of Differentiation, your job—from an organizational and an individual perspective—is only going to continue to increase in difficulty. However, if you start today to chart a fresh approach based on the Four Cornerstones of Distinction, you can begin to enhance your organization while you nurture and grow yourself.

Create differentiation.

Build distinction.

It will make all the difference.

A Final Thought

After my father passed away, my sister and I were standing by the casket, awaiting the beginning of visitation hours to greet friends and family as they paid their respects. Mark Adams, Crothersville's sole funeral home director, approached us with an amazed look on his face. "I've never seen anything like it," he told us. "The waiting line is really long to see your dad." Shelley and I made some generic comment, then the funeral director added, "You don't get it. The line wraps around the funeral home, then goes for blocks down the street! I've never seen anything like it!"

Many years after my family had sold our little grocery store, and a long time after Dad had moved away, our neighbors from a small country town still remembered the experience they received when they were his customers.

I can think of no better example. Develop a business of distinction. Create ultimate experiences for your customers—they will never forget you.

Resources

It is my hope and desire that you will continue to learn about strategic differentiation and what you can do to build distinction in the marketplace.

To that end, here is a list of resources—both in print and online—you may use to grow and share your knowledge. You'll find a more complete collection on the Web site for this book: http://CreateDistinction.com.

Outstanding Business and Professional Development Books

The One-Minute Entrepreneur: The Secret to Creating and Sustaining a Successful Business by Ken Blanchard, Don Hutson, and Ethan Willis (Doubleday Business)

Mastery: The Keys to Success and Long-Term Fulfillment by George Leonard (Plume)

Values-Based Financial Planning: The Art of Creating and Inspiring Financial Strategy by Bill Bachrach (Aim High Publishing)

The Tipping Point: How Little Things Can Make a Big Difference by Malcolm Gladwell (Back Bay Books)

My Father's Hand: A Daughter's Reflections on a Father's Wisdom by Naomi Rhode (Executive Books)

The Fred Factor by Mark Sanborn (Doubleday Business)

It's the Will, Not the Skill: Principles and Philosophies of Success by Jim Tunney (Success Publishing)

How to Be a Great Communicator: In Person, on Paper, and on the Podium by Nido Qubein (High Point University Press)

The SPEED of Trust: The One Thing That Changes Everything by Stephen M. R. Covey (Free Press)

The Eight Competencies of Relationship Selling: How to Reach the Top 1% in Just 15 Extra Minutes a Day by Jim Cathcart (Leading Authorities Press)

The Magic of Thinking Big by David Schwartz (Fireside)

*The Platinum Rule: Discover the Four Basic Business
Personalities and How They Can Lead You to Success* by
Tony Alessandra and Michael J. O'Connor (Grand
Central Publishing)

*The Voice of Authority: 10 Communication Strategies Every
Leader Needs to Know* by Dianna Booher (McGraw-Hill)

Service America in the New Economy by Karl Albrecht and
Ron Zemke (McGraw-Hill)

*Leadership Gold: Lessons I've Learned from a Lifetime of
Leading* by John Maxwell (Nelson Business)

Blogs

Here are a select few—of many—blogs I've discovered that deal
with differentiation and the customer experience. You'll find a
more complete list at http://CreateDistinction.com.

Differentiation Strategy

http://www.1000ventures.com/business_guide/
differentiation_strategy.html

Creating Differentiation

http://www.venturerepublic.com/resources/Brand_
community_brand_differentiation_leadership.asp

Branding Strategy

http://www.brandingstrategyinsider.com/2007/11/
creating-brands.html

The Expertise Marketplace

http://expertisemarketing.typepad.com/marketplace/
differentiation_positioning_branding/index.html

Ben Edwards's Marketing Blog

http://writemarketinggroup.blogspot.com/2005/03/
differentiation-is-key-to-real-success.html

Seth Godin's Blog

http://sethgodin.typepad.com/seths_blog/2004/04/
differentiation.html

Experience Solutions

http://www.experiencesolutions.co.uk/blog/category/
experience-design/

Customer Experience Matrix

http://customerexperiencematrix.blogspot.com/

Customer Experience Blog

http://maximumcustomerexperience.typepad.com/

Forrester

http://www.forrester.com/rb/search/results.jsp?N=50170

All Business

http://www.allbusiness.com/sales/customer-
service/10783-1.html

Customer Experience Matters

http://experiencematters.wordpress.com/

Blog Toplist

http://www.blogtoplist.com/rss/customer-service.html

Brand Blog

http://brand.blogs.com/mantra/customer_experience/
index.html

Duct Tape Marketing Blog

http://service.ducttapemarketing.com/

Service Untitled

http://www.serviceuntitled.com/category/customer-
service/

Customer Experience Center

http://www.customerexperiencecenter.org/

Passion for the Good Customer Experience
   http://p4tgce.blogspot.com/

Customer Service
   http://customerservice.blog.co.uk/

Client Service Blog
   http://www.clientservice.blogspot.com/

Shep Hyken
   http://shephyken.blogspot.com/

Customer Service King
   http://www.customerserviceking.com/category/
   customer-service/

Notes

Introduction

1. J. A. Pearce and J. B. Robinson, *Strategic Management: Formulation, Implementation and Control*, 8th ed. (New York: McGraw-Hill, 2003).

Chapter 1

1. Ron Waite, "Turbo Tennis," Tennis Server, August 2006, http://www.tennisserver.com.

2. Michael LeBoeuf, *How to Win Customers and Keep Them for Life*, rev. ed. (New York: Berkley Trade, 2000); GMP: *The Greatest Management Principle in the World* (New York: Putnam, 1985).

3. Eric Schlosser, *Fast Food Nation* (Boston: Houghton Mifflin, 2001).

4. Scott McKain, *What Customers REALLY Want* (Nashville: Thomas Nelson, 2006).

5. Jim Rohn

6. "Montgomery Ward," http://en.wikipedia.org/wiki/Montgomery_Ward.

Chapter 2

1. Ric Flair with Keith Elliot Greenberg, *Ric Flair: To Be the Man* (New York: Pocket Books, 2005).

2. Matt Krantz, *USA Today*, January 15, 2008.

3. Andrea Holecek, "The Dirt on Dry Cleaners," *Munster, Indiana, Times*, January 18, 2004.

4. Joe Edwards, *Nation's Restaurant News*, June 4, 1984.

Chapter 3

1. Michael Porter, *Competitive Advantage: Creating and Sustaining Superior Performance* (New York: Free Press, 1985).

2. Mark Gillies, *Automotive Magazine*, 2002.

3. Ron Jonash, *USA Today Magazine*, January 1, 2000.

4. Nick Churchouse, "Only One in Three Happy with Service," *The Press* (Christchurch, New Zealand), December 8, 2007.

5. EUCG, Inc., *PR Newswire* (Denver, Colorado), October 22, 2007.

Chapter 5

1. Janet Adamy, *Wall Street Journal*, February 27, 2008.

2. David Brody, CBN News broadcast, (http://www.cbn.com/CBNnews/475966.aspx) November 4, 2008.

3. Brian Hiatt and Evan Serpick, "The Record Industry's Decline," *Rolling Stone*, June 28, 2007, http://www.rollingstone.com.

Chapter 6

1. Alan G. Robinson and Sam Stern, *Corporate Creativity* (San Francisco: Berrett Koehler, 1998)

2. Bruce D. Airo, *Supervision* (a magazine with a sixty-year history that is, according to its Web site, "a monthly publication dedicated to providing the most timely and relevant information to today's supervisors and managers"), November 2006.

3. Ibid.

4. Stefi Weisburd, *Science News*, November 1987.

5. Bryan Ochalla, *Credit Union Management*, August 2003.

6. *R&D*, October 1988.

7. Ken Blanchard and Barbara Glanz, *The Simple Truths of Service: Inspired by Johnny the Bagger* (Blanchard Family Partnership, 2005).

8. William M. Luther, *The Marketing Plan: How to Prepare and Implement It*, 3rd ed. (New York: AMACOM, 2001), 120.

9. Andrei Codrescu, commentary aired on *All Things Considered*, September 21, 2001.

10. "Build Your Business Through Non-traditional Sales & Marketing Techniques," *Motor*, May 2005.

11. "Obama 2.0 Marketing," http://obama20marketing.blogspot.com

12. Wagner James Au, "Confirmed: Obama *Is* Campaigning on Xbox 360!, http://gigaom.com/2008/10/13/confirmed-obama-is-campaigning-on-xbox-360/

13. Dr. Jac Fitz-enz, *Human Resource Planning*, September 1993.

14. Jim Collins, *Good to Great* (New York: Collins, 2001).

15. Forbes.com, February 26, 2008.

16. Don Reisinger, C-net News, http://news.cnet.com/circuit-city-execs-killed-the-company/

17. Sandra M. Jones, "Walgreens open to change," Chicago Tribune, October 31, 2008

18. Forbes.com, February 26, 2008.

19. Collins, *Good to Great*.

20. David S. Hilzenrath, "Report Slams Fannie Mae: U.S. Regulators Find Accounting Failures at Housing Financier," *Washington Post*, September 23, 2004.

21. Andrea James, "Starbucks profit takes bitter shot for the year," *Seattle Post-Intelligencer*, November 11, 2008.

Chapter 7

1. Hilary McLellan of McLellan Wyatt Digital, http://www. tech-head.com.

2. Joseph Campbell, *The Hero with a Thousand Faces*, 2nd ed. (Novato, Calif.: New World Library, 2008); George Lucas statement appears in *A Fire in the Mind: The Life of Joseph Campbell* by Stephen and Robin Larsen (New York: Doubleday, 1991).

3. Ibid.

4. Excerpted from "Obama: Victory Speech," *New York Times*, November 5, 2008.

5. Mary E. Boyce, "Organizational Story and Storytelling: A Critical Review," *Journal of Organizational Change* (1996).

6. Peter Burrows, "The Mac in the Gray Flannel Suit," *Business Week*, May 12, 2008.

7. CNN report, September 28, 1998, http://www.cnn.com/ SHOWBIZ/Movies/9809/28/screen.test.

8. Ibid.

Chapter 8

1. Customers Are Always; http://www.customersarealways.com

2. Maria Palma, "What Is a Customer-Focused Strategy?" Customers Are Always, May 10, 2008, http://www. customersarealways.com/2008/05/what_is_a_ customerfocused_stra.html.

3. "Shared Belief in the 'Golden Rule,' or The Ethics of Reciprocity," ReligiousTolerance.org (the Web site of Ontario Consultants on Religious Tolerance), http://www.religioustolerance.org/aboutus.htm.

Acknowledgments

In every book I write and every speech I present, I make a specific point of acknowledging the extraordinary relationship I have with my best friend, Tim Durham, Chairman and CEO of Obsidian Enterprises. I am eternally thankful for his insight and counsel. It is my honor to serve as Vice Chairman of our organization—and, a special thanks to all of our Obsidian employees who work every day to create distinction for our organization.

This book is in your hands now because Joel Miller, Publisher at Nelson Business, believed in the concept when it was nothing more than a mere idea. I'm so appreciative of his passion and enthusiasm for this project—and for his savvy and positive critiques. Thom Chitton originally edited this manuscript with a commitment that was quite impressive. Heather Skelton took the ball and carried the project across the finish line. My sincere thanks to Jason Jones for his work in leading the effort to tell the world about this book. Scott Harris has been enthusiastic about marketing this book from the outset—and I am grateful. From the sales team to the graphic designers, we have all truly been partners in this project, and I am thankful to be associated with the incredible team at Thomas Nelson Publishers.

Every single day, I am grateful for the work of Shelley Erwin. She serves McKain Performance Group as the Vice President of Marketing, but is, in fact, our Chief Operating Officer, handling all of the day-to-day work, so I can write books and present speeches. (She's also my favorite—and *only*—sister!) Perry Cremans is our Director of Content Services, and creates "UCE's" for our clients, enabling us to show the world we "walk our talk."

No one could have better professional colleagues than I possess with my fellow members of Speakers Roundtable. Their generosity is amazing—and their friendship beyond description. It is such an honor to be a part of this group. Thanks, as well, to the speakers bureaus and my many clients across the country and around the world that keep my calendar full.

Heartfelt appreciation to the best friends a guy could have— my pals in the greatest band in the history of country music, Diamond Rio. Thanks to my best buddy Brian Prout, as well as

Dana Williams, Gene Johnson, Jimmy Olander, Dan Truman and Marty Roe. (And, road manager, Danny Beard!) Brian and Dana stood up with me at my wedding—and Marty sang, "The Lord's Prayer"—and the entire gang jammed for the reception! You guys rock! (But, not too much--you're a *country* band!)

I'm also appreciative of the support and my renewed friendship (after several decades) with the legendary Oak Ridge Boys. William Lee Golden has been a real mentor with his vision and integrity. It's hard to describe how much it means to me that he truly cares about our friendship! Richard Sterban is a model of hard work and dynamic manners. Duane Allen is the guy I always wanted to be when I was a teen—smooth, sophisticated, and polished. It's great to know that some things never change. Finally, there's not a better guy on the planet than Joe Bonsall. His books are inspirational, his stories compelling, and his talent limitless. He's a *true* friend. Thanks, too, to Darrick Kinslow—a great buddy who keeps the wheels going for one of the greatest acts in music history.

Thanks, as well, to Bruce Johnston—my longtime top friend and colleague—formerly the CEO for Old Mutual Investment Partners and my partner in The Value Added Institute. There's no one around who challenges my philosophies more than him—a true visionary thinker, and flat out the best leader I have ever worked for and with. Kudos, too, to Ted Greene at Modern Management for his years of partnership and Mel Berger at William Morris Agency for giving me a first chance at being an author.

A special thank you to Greg Daniel of Daniel Literary Agency for taking this project on, and seeing it through to completion. This is the beginning of a terrific relationship!

Saving the best for last, I'm most grateful to a wonderful woman who was willing to take a chance on this lost soul and worried widower at a time that I wasn't at my best. My bride, Tammy, somehow believed in me to the point that she moved from her hometown and allowed me to share the life that she had built with her two wonderful sons. Even though I make my living with words, I find myself ill-equipped to describe how grateful I am that you are my partner and in my life...every day. I love you.

And to all of **YOU**...thank you for reading. My sincere desire is that your time and effort has been well spent with *The Collapse of Distinction*.

Scott McKain

November 4, 2008

Indianapolis, Indiana

About the Author

Scott McKain is vice chairman of Obsidian Enterprises, a dynamic holding company with nineteen diverse affiliated businesses generating more than $100 million in annual revenue, and vice chairman of Durham Capital Corporation. He is chairman of McKain Performance Group, Inc., a highly successful company specializing in educating visionary organizations and professionals on business growth through strategic differentiation. He is also cofounder and principal of the Value Added Institute, a think tank that focuses on the growth of client retention and acquisition through enhanced customer experiences.

Scott McKain's calling is business, but his passion is the platform. He presents compelling programs on creating distinction in the marketplace through the development of an Ultimate Customer Experience to visionary organizations that seek to expand their impact and profitability.

Scott McKain is the author of two highly successful business books, *ALL Business Is Show Business* and *What Customers REALLY Want,* both published by Thomas Nelson. He is a member of the Professional Speakers Hall of Fame and of Speakers Roundtable—a historic and elite association of twenty professional speakers and consultants, recognized as the market leaders in their respective fields.

From thousands of nominees, he was selected as one of ten Hoosier Heroes for his commitment to charitable involvement and philanthropy.

Scott lives with his wife, Tammy, and sons Corbin and Faron Byler in suburban Indianapolis, Indiana.

Contact:

Shelley Erwin, Vice President of Marketing

McKain Performance Group, Inc.

111 Monument Circle; Suite 4800

Indianapolis, IN 46204

800-838-6980

contact@ScottMcKain.com

www.ScottMcKain.com

www.UltimateCustomerExperience.com

Index